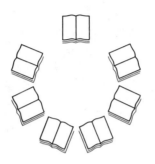

The Junior Great Books
Reading and Discussion
Program

JUNIOR GREAT BOOKS

Series Six, Volume Two
Second Semester

A Program of Interpretive Reading and Discussion

The Great Books Foundation
a nonprofit educational corporation

Published and distributed by
The Great Books Foundation
a nonprofit educational corporation
40 East Huron Street
Chicago, Illinois 60611

Acknowledgments

All possible care has been taken to trace ownership and secure permission for each selection in this series. The Great Books Foundation wishes to thank the following authors, publishers, and representatives for permission to reprint copyrighted material:

Raymond's Run, by Toni Cade Bambara, from GORILLA, MY LOVE. Copyright 1970 by Toni Cade Bambara. Reprinted by permission of Random House, Inc.

I Just Kept On Smiling, by Simon Burt, from FLORAL STREET. Copyright 1983, 1986 by Simon Burt. Reprinted by permission of Curtis Brown Ltd.

Star Food, by Ethan Canin, from EMPEROR OF THE AIR. Copyright 1988 by Ethan Canin. Reprinted by permission of Houghton Mifflin Company.

The Sand Castle, by Mary Lavin, from COLLECTED STORIES BY MARY LAVIN. Copyright 1971 by Mary Lavin. Reprinted by permission of the author.

The Last Great Snake, by Mary Q. Steele, from THE OWL'S KISS. Copyright 1978 by Mary Q. Steele. Reprinted by permission of Greenwillow Books, a division of William Morrow & Company.

The Secret Lion, by Alberto Alvaro Rios, from THE IGUANA KILLER. Copyright 1984 by Alberto Alvaro Rios. Reprinted by permission of Confluence Press.

Soumchi, by Amos Oz. Copyright 1978 by Amos Oz and Am Oved Publishers Ltd., Tel Aviv. English translation copyright 1980 by Chatto & Windus Ltd. Reprinted by permission of Deborah Owen Ltd.

Cover illustrations by Leo and Diane Dillon.

Contents

The Last Great Snake

Mary Q. Steele

Bala was sitting by his fireside, carefully polishing his spearhead, when Gatani appeared in the circle of light. Bala stared at him and said nothing.

"I have come for my magic stone," said Gatani at last.

"Have you indeed?" responded Bala. He rubbed sand furiously along the edge of his spearhead.

Gatani was silent. He seemed to be waiting. Bala did not look at him. When Gatani spoke again, his voice was cold with anger. "You have stolen my magic stone. Everyone knows you have stolen it. And now I have come for it."

Bala continued to polish the spear with much energy. When he was done with one side, he turned it over.

"I have not stolen your stone," he answered evenly. "What everyone knows and what is true are not always the same thing. I know nothing of your stone. I have not seen it."

Gatani clenched his fists. His breath hissed between his lips. "The stone was in my house," he whispered. "Now it is gone. Three people saw you leave my house. Three people. Only you could have taken my magic stone."

His eyes blazed above the fire. Then he turned and walked away into the darkness.

Bala went on with his polishing.

In the morning he went to the market, for he had some skins to trade. Anyway he always went to the market on those mornings when he did not hunt. It was a good time to see his friends and hear whatever news there was to hear. He sat down in his usual place, but no one came to ask about his pelts, though Bala and his wife had prepared them carefully.

Bala's wife wished to trade for seeds for her garden and the stuff with which to make a new fish net and perhaps a small metal ornament for her little daughter's neck.

The people in the market did not speak to Bala. Many even turned their heads and would not look at him. He sat a long time and no one came to trade with him.

Then he knew in fact that his honor was gone and everyone truly believed he had stolen Gatani's magic stone.

He gathered up his skins and carried them back to his home and laid them on a shelf. He took two or three tubers and some bread and his spear and his knife and walked away.

He did not speak to anyone and there were few to see him go, for those who were not hunting or gardening were at the market.

Bala did not say good-bye to his wife and his son and daughter. His wife would be working with her plants and her children would be with her. She need not look again upon her husband, a man without honor.

Her father and brothers would help her and soon people would forget. Perhaps someday another man would marry her. It seemed unlikely. Another man would not want the care of Bala's children, the son and daughter of the one who had stolen Gatani's magic stone.

Bala did not walk on the trail, for he did not want to meet anyone. He walked well away from the marked path, among the trees. And he went quietly, so that no one would hear him, so that he might hear others coming toward him in time to shelter himself behind a tree.

He had no wish to look into the face of anyone who supposed that Bala would do such a thing, would steal anything at all, much less Gatani's magic stone. The stone was not really Gatani's. It had come to him from his grandfather, who had been dead for many years.

Who would steal from an old dead man?

Bala walked softly and thought about the magic stone, which had lain in a carved box in Gatani's house ever since the old man died. No one but Gatani and a few of the honored old men of the village had seen it. It was said to be a clear and colorless stone and in its depth one could see true things, what had been and what was to come.

Gatani fed it every week with the blood of certain animals, mixed with fresh spring water. Sometimes he dared to look into its depths and see the truth, what had been and

what was to come. He did not do it often. It was a dangerous thing to do, for the truth might crack a heart or make
a brain go numb forever.

Bala saw a hare among the bushes and killed it with his
spear to eat for supper. He was a good hunter. His family
had never lacked for meat or hides. He had no reason to
steal, not even a magic stone.

He picked up the hare and looked at it. Yet he had indeed gone into Gatani's house. Gatani's wife had no sense.
She had left her fish lying by the door and gone away. Bala
had watched and waited for her to come back, and when a
crow flew down to eat the catch, Bala had frightened it off
and himself taken the fish inside the house and laid them
on the hearth.

Three people were passing when he came out and no
one thought it strange.

Only the next day, when Gatani opened the carved box
to feed the stone and discovered that it was missing, only
then had three people come forward and told how Bala had
been alone in Gatani's house. Had gone inside when
Gatani was away hunting and his wife gone to fetch water
to boil her fish.

Bala was angry with these people and yet he knew they
had done what they thought was right. To steal was a
dreadful thing. And to steal a magic stone was more dreadful still.

A magic stone, a clear and flashing crystal from the head
of the giant snake Conokili, a stone which had once caused
rain to fall when the forests were almost parched to powder

and the gardens yielding nothing.

Bala could remember that terrible year himself, though he had been very young at the time. The stone's rightful owner, Gatani's grandfather, had done that terrifying thing, had dared to go to the stone and ask that it make the rain fall and the thunder roll. But then Gatani's grandfather had been a man of huge courage anyway, for he had killed the giant snake Conokili and taken the stone from its head in the first place.

Bala walked on, deeper and deeper into the forest. When night fell he made a small fire and cooked his supper. And when he had polished his spear carefully, he lay down and went to sleep and over his head passed the silent stars and a dark moon.

But in his house in the village his wife lay awake and heard the cry of owls, for she did not believe that Bala was a man who had stolen a magic crystal.

Nevertheless, she knew that in leaving he had done the only thing he could do, and she spent that night in sorrow for him and for herself and for their children. In the early morning she rose and went a little way into the forest and buried the skins he had left on the shelf.

But she did not forget the spot where they lay, and it was a little as if she had buried Bala there. And sometimes she would come and stand awhile near the place and sometimes she brought her son and daughter with her.

In four days her father came to take them away to live with him in his house. But she would not go.

"I will stay here," she told him.

Her father was a kind man and he saw that she wished to stay in her own house with her memories and her hope that Bala would someday return there. Yet he was a proud man and knew that if she went on living there alone, everyone in the village would mark it. They would remember Bala and what he had done and that she had been wife to a man who had lost his honor.

So her father went away in some anger, but every week he brought her meat from his hunting and asked if she needed anything.

And time went by.

Day after day Bala walked deeper into the forest, farther and farther away from his home. He endured many hardships. He did not think about his family often, for he had made up his mind not to. He was a man without honor and he had no right to long for his home and his family.

After weeks of journeying, he emerged from the forest and found himself in a long valley of green grasses. In the distance he could see strange formations of dull white rocks. He walked toward the nearest of them and saw with shock that they were not rocks at all. In the grass lay bones, enormous bones, the bones of some animal far bigger than any creature Bala had ever seen. Rib bones taller than himself and teeth bigger than his fist and long, long tusks.

He was filled with fear and thought to leave this valley. But it was a pleasant green place, the grass was soft and deep, rabbits and birds were there in plenty. So he stayed.

And after a while he knew that he had been meant to find

this place and live there. For a man without honor is like a bone stripped of its flesh and this should be his home from now on. He would be a bone and live among bones.

There were a few small springs here and there. Rushes grew around them and insects hovered over them. Bala chose the biggest and clearest of these springs and made his fire nearby.

Although it was warm and he had no trouble finding food, he knew that winter would come and with it cold weather and rain or snow. He built a house, using the awesome bones. He made a hut by standing some of the rib bones up and leaning them against each other in a sort of circle. And then he wound grasses and reeds in and out of the bones and plastered the whole thing over with mud and more grass, and he fashioned a door of skins.

He found a rock for the hearth in the middle of the house and there was a hole in the center of the roof, where the rib bones did not quite meet, and out of this hole the smoke from his hearth could drift up into the open sky.

When it was done, it was a good house, and he went inside and kindled a small fire and sat by it and polished his spear and whetted his knife.

But when it came time to sleep, he went outside and lay on the ground, for he did not yet feel easy in his house of bones. Only when the weather grew so cold that he could not sleep comfortably did he begin to spend his nights indoors.

And he waited for whatever would happen next.

When the first snow fell, he rose from his bed and went

out his skin door into the world which had changed, since he first came here, from green to brown to white. The huge bones looked lusterless and weatherbeaten and ancient, looming up in the snow. They looked almost tan against the new whiteness.

He wondered what dreadful animals had come here to die and leave their skeletons for him to find. He wondered if anyone else knew of this valley and if other people ever came here.

Almost at once a man appeared, a man older than himself, with a tired, thin face and stringy arms. A hunter with a spear. But the spear was not polished and sharp-edged and shining, like Bala's. It was dull and useless-looking.

The two stood staring at each other, and at last the older man spoke.

"I have come here searching for game," he said. "I see you have come here to live." He nodded at Bala's hut.

Bala was polite. "I did not mean to intrude on land belonging to others," he replied. "I have seen no one except you since I have been here. I will leave if this is a place where I should not have made my dwelling."

The man smiled a little. "This place belongs to no one but the bones of the great creatures which once lived and died here. Many believe that it belongs to their ghosts or to evil witches or bad spirits. I do not know of anyone who wants to live here except yourself. I come here to hunt. I am no longer young and my eyes trouble me. To find meat and skins for my family grows harder and harder. Here there are rabbits at least. And sometimes deer and other things. When I come home empty-handed for many days, then I travel to this place and hunt where few others hunt. I usually kill something."

"Have you no sons to hunt for you?" asked Bala.

The man shook his head. "My wife and my two sons died many years ago, in a plague," he answered. "And then when I was too old, foolishly I married again and my new wife and I have a young daughter, but no sons. My wife is a good and patient woman, she works hard in the garden, she fishes and sometimes she traps birds. But we are in need of skins. And other things."

He hesitated and then went on sadly, "Our village is small. And somehow we do not seem to have many children. Not enough to take care of all of us who are growing old. We try to help each other out. I do what I can."

Bala felt sorry for the other man. And yet he had not lost his honor. He was still part of his village.

But Bala said nothing of his own troubles and why he was here. It was too terrible a thing to say aloud. Not yet.

"We will hunt together, you and I," he said. "I know where we can find deer. I do not need so much meat. I will share whatever we find and you may have the skin. I am not in need of skins."

The other man bowed his head.

"You are kind," he replied. "But I have seen the deer's tracks in the snow. I will hunt alone today. If I have no luck, tomorrow perhaps I can go with you."

Bala saw how it was. This man wanted to hunt for his family by himself. He did not want the company of a stranger, one who lived in this queer valley full of bones and ghosts. He perhaps could sense that Bala was a man who had lost his honor.

The man walked away. The sun came out and most of the snow melted. Bala busied himself at his few tasks. He killed a hare.

In the evening the other man returned, but he had no deer with him. "I lost their tracks when the snow melted," he said. "I searched a long time and I did not find them again."

"Share my supper," said Bala. "It is too much for one and I have no trouble getting hares and rabbits. They are all about."

"Thank you," said the other man.

He came in Bala's house and laid his spear to one side and sat by the hearth. They ate in silence and then once again Bala polished and sharpened his spear. To make talk, he told the man how he had once heard of a town that had been threatened by a great beast.

"Do you suppose it might be such a beast as died here?" Bala asked.

The man considered. "Perhaps," he answered. "I have never heard of one being seen alive. But that is no reason to believe they do not exist. The world is full of wonders no one has ever seen. There are some who say the great snake Ulukini lives in the hills to the north of this valley still. One last giant snake with a magic crystal in its head."

Bala's heart beat fast. Did this man know who he was and that everyone supposed him to be the thief of Gatani's magic stone? But his hands went on polishing and polishing, smoothly and quickly, and did not falter.

"As you say, there are many strange things in the world," he said at last.

He laid down his spear and picked up the other man's. As though in absent-mindedness he polished it too, until it glistened and the edges were sharp and keen. Then he lay down and went to sleep.

The next morning there was more snow. The two hunted together and before noon each had killed a small deer.

"I have meat and skins in plenty," Bala told the other man. "You may take my deer to your family. I would not want to waste so much, and so much would waste if I were to keep it."

Again the man bent his head and did not look at Bala. "I am grateful," he responded. "You are a very kind man."

He said nothing more but kept his eyes on the ground so that Bala might not read there the question he did not speak: Why are you living alone in this strange place of long-dead beasts and ghosts?

He went away, carrying the two deer, and Bala watched him go.

And time went by.

The winter was not very cold or very long, and soon the grass grew up and turned green among the bones and bright flowers blossomed here and there. Bala busied himself as best he could. He grew used to his surroundings and it no longer seemed so curious and uncanny to live in a house made of enormous ribs or to stumble over a vast tusk half-buried in the earth.

Yet it was lonely still and grew no less lonely. And Bala had every day to make his mind turn away from thoughts of his wife and children, of his home and his friends in the market place.

He missed too the tasseled trees of spring and the returning birds, for in this valley there were few trees and only small ones. And the birds were not the soaring singing birds of the forest but mostly ground birds with quiet sad voices and dim colors.

Some days he walked the long distance to the hills toward the north to stand among the big trees and watch their new leaves unfolding and to see the birds, scarlet and blue and green, which flew among the branches. And he would look up and think about the giant snake which lived in the peaks of the mountains, with a magic stone like Gatani's in its head.

And time went by.

And then one morning he woke and stood up and looked about him. Now that the weather was warm he once again slept in the open, unless it rained. Two figures were coming toward him across the green grasses of the valley. He waited, and when they came closer, he saw that it was an old woman and a boy, a boy about fourteen years old.

They did not come to him but stopped some way off. They saw him, he was quite sure, and he wondered why they did not walk closer to look at him and perhaps speak to him, but they did not.

They made a sort of camp and for two days they lived there without appearing to pay him any attention. He was tempted to go to them, to offer them some of the hares and rabbits and birds he killed for food. He did not go. He was a man without honor and must wait for others to come to him.

At last the old woman approached his house one afternoon. She did not speak. She walked about his house several times, inspecting it carefully. She even lifted the skin door and peered inside.

Then she went away.

During the next few days she and the boy worked together and made themselves a similar hut of rib bones and mud and grass. It was not so good a house as Bala's and again he bethought himself to go to offer help. Not until he saw the old woman struggling to carry in a hearthstone did he travel the distance to their home and take the stone from her and carry it inside and place it where it should go and settle it into the earth.

They did not speak, not even when he went outside and rearranged some of the grasses and mud and reeds in some places to make the walls more weather-resistant. When he was done, he stepped back and looked it over, and then the old woman addressed him.

"I give you thanks," she said. "Your help was needed. I am old and my grandson is young and we neither of us have the strength for doing such tasks properly."

"Why did you not ask for my help?" asked Bala. "I am a grown man and strong and have little to do with my time. I would have liked helping you make your house."

The old woman fell silent once again. She gazed off into the west, in the direction from which they had come. Her hair was long and tangled and her clothes were worn and tattered and hung in ragged streamers about her knees.

Finally she said, "When we came here, I thought we should be alone. I did not think that someone else would be living here. It is best that my grandson and I have nothing to do with other people. I knew of no other place to go, so we stayed here. But I thought it wisest to act as if we were alone here. To act as if you were some kind of harmless beast living nearby and to treat you thus. When we have been here longer, perhaps I will think of some way we can be neighbors, even friends. But not yet."

"My name is Bala," said Bala. "I can hunt for you. I am a good hunter. I can supply meat and skins for you, at least."

"My grandson is a good hunter too," replied the old woman. "And I can catch birds and lizards and such. We do not lack. We can provide for ourselves."

She turned away and Bala walked back to his house, having been dismissed.

Still every day he watched them and wondered about them and why they were here. Such a woman, an old brave woman—for courage stood in every line of her face—such a woman must be here for some purpose. She had come here not because she must but because she wanted to.

And why had she brought her grandson with her? To provide her with food and skins and shelter? No, such an old woman would prefer taking her chances on dying alone or living on her own resources.

There must be some other reason why the boy was with her.

Bala wondered and wondered, and was glad to have something to wonder about. Was pleased to wake in the mornings and see the two small figures moving about among the great leg bones of long-dead beasts, two other human beings here in this valley with him for whatever mysterious purpose.

He watched the grandson go off with his spear and come back with food. He watched the old woman making a fire and cooking their meals and treating the skins of deer and hare.

They too slept outside, for the weather was warm and pleasant, and Bala supposed the others must feel, as he had done at first, uneasy about sleeping in their house of bones.

When bad weather forced them all to sleep inside, Bala noticed a curious thing. When the old woman emerged after the rain was over, she danced. She stamped and leaped and twisted; her long hair and tattered clothes flew about her like the branches of a storm-tossed tree.

Bala did not like to watch. She danced for some design of her own making, secret and important. He was intruding when he watched. But he could not turn his eyes away and watched until she stopped at last and stood for a long time with bowed head.

With all his heart Bala longed to know her. Still he

waited. He dared not be the one to come forward.

And then one day when Bala was stalking a deer, he came face to face with the grandson. The boy must have been hunting the same deer and somehow they had not seen each other, so intent was each on his prey, until they were almost upon one another.

The boy was big, though not yet full grown. He was well made and handsome, and his clothes, unlike his grandmother's, were clean and whole and tidily kept.

Only his eyes bothered Bala, for there was, far in their depths, something sly and more than sly, dangerous and fearsome. Like his grandmother this boy had great courage, but unlike her he did not know the proper way to use it.

Or he did not want perhaps to use it in the proper way.

Now he smiled, but whatever dwelt deep inside him did not go away with the smile. It stayed there still, cold and hard and somehow more fearsome because of the smile.

"We have both lost our quarry," he said, for the deer had bounded away.

"There are more deer," answered Bala. "And hares and rabbits and birds."

The boy nodded indifferently. "We do not need food anyway," he continued. "I hunt because there is little else for me to do. My grandmother can spend her hours sitting in the sun and be happy. But I am young and must move about. Better the company of hares than the company of an old woman who would rather speak to her memories than to me."

Bala was moved to ask the boy to hunt with him. He too

longed for companionship and a way to occupy his days.

Yet he recalled the old woman's words. She had spoken the truth, he was sure. It was best that she and this boy not be his friends or even his neighbors for a time.

"My name is Bala," he said at length. "If you need my help, you have only to ask."

The boy smiled again. "I am Medana and my grandmother is called Kotil," he said.

And Bala went away, as though he must hunt further.

After that he sometimes saw the boy raise his arm in greeting in the mornings. The boy and the old woman watched him too, then, and wondered why he was here.

One evening not many days later the old woman came to Bala's campfire.

"I see you keep well," she said. "I am glad." She paused. "I see that you do not want to say why you are here or how long you mean to stay. I do not want to press you. But I have come to tell you why I am here, for I have watched my grandson hail you in the morning, and sooner or later he will find a way to meet you again, when I cannot prevent the meeting. Someday when you travel north to the trees he will follow you. Or he will go before you and wait for you to come to him."

She stopped once more and stared into the fire. Bala could see that she was reluctant to say what she had to say.

"There is something the matter with my grandson. I do not know what it is," she went on. "It is an evil that lives inside his head. He does not do bad things himself. It is rather that he makes others do bad things. He has a way. He knows how to give another person the notion to do what he or she should not do, so that other person must take the blame. I have come here with him, for I know a little magic and I am trying to cure him. If I cannot cure him, at least I will keep him from harming others. That is why I have brought him here. I have made a chain between him and me, a strong chain. He can wander, but he cannot leave me. Still he can reach you. I give you this warning. Whatever your reason for being here, do not let him discover it."

Bala knew then that Kotil herself had learned in some way why he was here. She knew that he was a man who had lost his honor and with it his family and friends.

She knew that he longed to be once more at home with the people he loved, to have life be as it had once been for him. And that he must use all his strength to put those longings from his heart.

And in turn he sensed something about Kotil. He knew why she did her strange dance. She could not spend a night shut up with Medana's evil without running a risk of being defiled by it. Therefore on those mornings she danced away the bad effects of having spent long hours imprisoned with her grandson.

Bala knew that magic dances were very powerful and he had heard often how they could be used to cleanse and purify. He was again ashamed that he had watched her dance, a ritual which she should have been allowed to perform in privacy.

Now he said, "I am grateful for your warning. I will heed it."

She went away and that day Bala did not hunt but sat by

his house and pondered.

And in the next few days he kept a diligent watch and often saw Medana following him or waiting for him a long way ahead. Bala no longer walked to the forests at the northern head of the valley, not simply because he was afraid of meeting Medana, but because the year was growing dry and hot. In the woodlands the leaves hung limp upon the trees and the birds seldom sang or even showed themselves.

Hunting became a real task, not something done to pass the time but something done because birds and hares were scarce, and once or twice Bala went supperless to bed.

He hunted now farther and more intensely than he had before, and it was thus that he forgot Kotil's warning and allowed Medana to find him, waiting for rabbits, crouched in the grass; in grass now turned brown and dry, so crisp it crackled underfoot and made hunting even more difficult.

Yet Medana was able to come silently up to him. Bala had observed before that Medana could move as quietly as a shadow.

"I have killed a deer," Medana announced. "We will share it with you, if you like."

Bala hesitated. He was hot and weary and would have liked some of the deer meat. Yet he answered, "No, I will soon have my rabbits. You and your grandmother will need all the meat of your deer for yourselves. I thank you."

"Very well," Medana said. He smiled and gave a small shrug. "You have been talking to my grandmother, I believe, for you have done your best to avoid me. I know. I have seen you turn aside when I came near."

Bala said nothing to this. He could not deny it.

Medana went on. "She has told you that she believes I am an evil person. Now I will tell you something about my grandmother. She speaks the truth, for she has taken a vow that she will never lie. And if you ask her any question, she must tell you the truth if she knows it. It was a very solemn vow."

"Then you are an evil person and she was right to warn me against you," said Bala abruptly.

"So she believes," Medana answered. He smiled again and went away.

By long effort Bala killed two grouse for his supper. He went back to his house and turned over in his mind what Medana had told him.

The next day he determined to go once more to the north forests. Surely he could find a deer there if he climbed high enough into the hills. There would still be much forage under the branches of the great trees and there would still be water in the streams. No doubt many had fled there and Bala would follow.

He set out early and made certain that Medana did not see him go. He kept a careful watch and saw no sign of the boy.

It was a long journey and at its end the shade of the trees was welcome and the long slope of the hills urged him farther and farther in among them, toward the peaks where the giant snake Ulukini lay hidden.

Was it true? Did one last, enormous serpent lie somewhere among those distant ridges?

Bala turned back quickly and, when he had killed his deer, left the forest hurriedly, not glancing back. Medana was waiting for him at the edge of the valley and walked with him.

"I have not killed anything for my grandmother and me to eat today," Medana said. "It is good that we still have some of the meat from the deer."

"Yes," answered Bala. "Though I am ever willing to share with you anything that I have."

"And we with you," murmured Medana.

They walked on and Medana asked, "Have you lived here always?" and Bala answered, "Almost always."

For it was almost so. His life in the village he had put behind him and he did not think of it if he could avoid it.

"Would you not like to go back there, where you came from?" Medana pressed him. "You must be far from where you were born. I am sure it is so. I asked my grandmother and she said it was so. She is old and wise and knows much. And she must always speak the truth."

Bala walked on but at last said, "This is where I live now."

And he hastened his steps and left Medana behind.

Yet he turned his head once and looked back up at the mountains where the last giant snake lay sleeping in the sun. Perhaps.

And time went by.

The drought was long and hard, and one day the old woman and the boy came with a leather bottle and Kotil requested some water to drink, for their own spring had grown muddy and foul.

Though the spring near Bala's hut no longer bubbled up strongly, the water was still fairly clean and fresh. He filled their bottle and handed it to the old woman. "The rain is not far off," he told her. "I think we will soon have rain."

She shook her head. "No," she told him. "There will be no rain till days have passed more than the fingers of my two hands. We will have to do with what we have, with your help."

Medana gave his grandmother a cunning look. He turned suddenly and stared northward toward the hills. Bala followed his glance.

"There will be water in the hills, high up," Bala said. "Perhaps I could travel there and fetch some back for us."

"It is best not to travel in the hills," answered Kotil sharply. "There are many spirits in the hills and some of them dislike humankind and do not want our presence among them."

She turned away, but Bala took her arm.

"I have heard that one last great snake, Ulukini, one of those who bear a magic crystal in the skull, lives up in the mountains. Is it true?" he asked.

Kotil gave Bala and Medana both a sullen look.

"Yes, it is true," she answered finally. "The last great snake."

She and Medana walked back to their house and Bala

watched them go and a plan formed in his mind. Or not a plan, a thought for making a plan. It worried him, and in the nights throbbing with heat he lay awake and stared at the hazy stars and talked with himself as though he were two different people, with different views and feelings and even lives.

The dry weather continued, as Kotil had said it would, and Bala's spring dwindled. At last he arose one morning and walked to Kotil's house.

"My spring will soon be gone," he told her. "It is scarcely more than a trickle. If you will lend me your leather bottles, I will go into the hills and bring back enough water for us to drink until the rains come. Otherwise we may die."

Kotil stared at him strangely, but she brought out her three leather bottles. Bala had not thought to make one for himself, although he dressed his deerskins with as much care and skill as if he was intending to sell them in the market place. His wife, when he had a wife, had made their bottles and he was not sure he possessed the craft and quickness of hand to do it himself.

"Do not go too far," Kotil warned him. "And be very careful. Watch all you do."

"I will be careful," Bala promised.

He took the bottles and set out. He walked quickly though the day was hot and no wind stirred across the valley. When he came to the forest, he went at once to a place where he had, earlier in the year, found a small stream.

The stream was dry now and the moss on the stones had turned black and the ferns had died. He followed the dry bed up and up, and soon there was a little moisture among the rocks. And then a little higher a tiny rill.

He climbed and climbed and at last came to a real brook, and not much farther on to the source of the brook, a spring tumbling out from between two stones.

Bala set his bottles down at that spot. He drank and the water was sweet and cool. And then he went on.

There was no sign that any man had ever been here before, and he left a trail of sorts by which to find his way back quickly—a broken twig, a little pile of pebbles, a knife mark on a tree trunk.

But there was no sign either of the great snake Ulukini and at last he turned back.

He found the bottles and filled them and carried them as carefully as he could down the hillside and out of the forest. Kotil and Medana came to meet him.

"You have been gone a long time," said the old woman.

"Yes," answered Bala. "The spring was far up in the ridges. And I traveled back slowly. I did not want to drop the bottles. As it is, I have not brought back a great deal of water."

"It will suffice," said Kotil. "In two days we will have some rain and then in another two days much rain, more than we will want."

Bala did not look at the old woman, for he knew she would see in his eyes the reason he had been gone so long. She was a very wise woman, and no doubt she would know all he had been thinking during the sleepless nights when he had watched the stars and found himself two people warring one against the other.

"Did you see any signs of the spirits who live among the ridges?" asked Medana. "The ones my grandmother warned you about?"

"I saw nothing," Bala answered honestly.

"Did you see signs of the great serpent?" Medana's voice was mocking.

"I saw nothing," repeated Bala. He picked up one of the bottles and with it returned to his house.

The old woman had predicted rightly. In two days there were showers and then in another two days rain and rain, unending, endless.

And then there was a calamity. The house of Medana and Kotil, not so well built and sturdy as Bala's, collapsed. Bala saw it happen, saw the bones slowly slide away and topple. He ran at once and pulled the old woman from the wreckage and helped her to her feet. She was not injured, only a little frightened.

Medana was not inside, having gone to look at a trap for hares which he had set some days before. When he returned, he and Bala searched the ruins for the leather bottles and some skins.

"We will have to live together in Bala's house," said Kotil reluctantly. "The rain will end soon and we will rebuild our house."

It was crowded for three people in Bala's small shelter. There was little to eat and no dry wood for a fire. Kotil sang most of the day in a low, sad murmur and Bala thought she must do it to keep Medana's evil at bay, for she could not do her dance.

Bala himself often walked in the pouring rain rather than sit crushed together with the others in the house of bones, listening to the old woman's cracked voice going on and on. Sometimes Medana came with him. They would walk the length of the valley and back, looking for birds and rabbits. They found no great plenty, but enough.

And at last the weather changed and the sun shone once again and a steamy heat rose from the earth.

But before that happened the damage had been done. Two nights before the rain ended, Bala came back to his house with a hare from Medana's trap and enough twigs and grass to build a smoldering fire to cook the hare. Medana was pleased that his snare had succeeded at last and Kotil was glad of the fire, however small. Her bones ached from the damp.

Only Bala was discontent, sorry that Medana and not he had supplied the meal, sorry that he must share his house and the smoky air with this lean old woman and her grandson. Perhaps he had grown overaccustomed to living alone.

That was how the evil slipped in, he knew later. When he had allowed himself to be angry and troubled and fretted by little and foolish things, then even Kotil's songs and charms could not protect him. Medana must have known the moment had come.

"Today when I was out," Medana said suddenly, "the sun broke through the clouds. For just a breath it lit the mountain tops. Tell us, Grandmother, about the spirits there and what would happen to someone who climbed to the places where they stay."

"They are not to be spoken of lightly," she answered and her voice was curt. "And I know little about them, simply that they are there and some are good to humans and some are not, and if one goes among them one must go with care and protect oneself as best one can."

"Then tell us about the giant snake Ulukini and the wonder-working stone in its head," Medana urged in his sly voice.

Kotil sighed, rubbing her knees.

"Everyone knows," she said. "Seven of them were created. Seven giant serpents, each with a marvelous crystal in its head. They came into the world at its very beginning and they were meant to live until the world should end. Men have killed six of them and now there is only Ulukini left."

"How could they live until the end of the world?" asked Bala. "If men can kill them, cannot other things destroy them?"

"No," she replied. "Only men can find the one vulnerable spot. Only men have the knowledge to kill them and the sharp spear points which can be used against them."

Medana did not look at Kotil. He kept his eyes on Bala, and at last Bala asked, "What is the spot where the spear can enter?"

Kotil gazed into the fire for a long time. And then she said sadly, "Behind the head. Between the third and fourth row of scales. But it is wicked to speak of such things. The last great snake Ulukini is safe upon its mountaintop and should remain so."

She seized Medana by his chin and turned his head so that he must stare into her eyes or drop his lids. "Know this. The blood of the giant snake is poisonous," she cried harshly. "Should anyone thrust his spear into that vital spot, the blood would gush forth and he would die!"

Bala was astonished. How had Gatani's grandfather escaped such a fate? He must have been clever as well as brave. Bala was not clever or brave.

Medana did not turn his eyes from his grandmother's. He stared boldly and smiled his small smile and said softly, "Six of the great snakes have been killed, Grandmother. There must be a way."

And the sun shone at last and the grass grew green once again. Bala lived once again alone in his house. He did not go to help Kotil and Medana rebuild their shelter and they came no more to ask for water from his spring or any other thing. And Bala was lonely once more and without much to occupy his hands or his heart and so he spent long hours looking up into the mountains and wondering. And his thoughts went ever and again to the great serpent Ulukini and the stone in its head.

He reminded himself that he was neither brave nor clever.

The days had begun to shorten. Bala woke one morning before light. He rose and took his spear and his knife and some hides and a little food and set out toward the north, toward the forested ridges. As when he had left his wife and children he had tried not to look behind, so now he tried not to look ahead.

He remembered Kotil's words about the unfriendly spirits in the ridges. He had no weapon against them. He stopped and almost turned back, for his fear was great. And in the end he made himself go forward and thought only about walking, putting one foot in front of the other and walking and walking.

When he came into the forest, he followed the stream, now full and gushing, where he had got water in the dry season. He found beyond it some of the traces he had made for himself at that time. By nightfall he was far above the point he had reached before and lay down and slept where weariness overcame him.

In the morning he was hungry and ate what he had brought with him, for he was afraid of killing any of the birds or animals he saw in the undergrowth. Who knew whether such killing might not anger the spirits around him? Who knew indeed anything about these tall peaks and the dark trees which grew along them or what he might do to offend the invisible things which lived among them?

He began to climb again, and as the day went on and all he saw seemed not so different from what he had seen in other mountain forests, he made up his mind not to tremble as he had trembled before. Whatever befell him, befell him, and since he could not foresee it, he would try not to fear it but simply wait for it to happen.

And nothing happened.

He climbed up and down the ridges, always going higher when he could. And that evening he killed a hare for his supper and built a fire, and when he had eaten, polished his spear as had always been his custom. If any spirit wished to harm him, it could find him at any time, in daylight or in darkness. And so he slept and no harm came to him.

Once in a while as he journeyed he had a curious sensation of being surrounded by watching eyes. Did these beings know why he had come? And did they know that a terrible fate awaited him? And did they stay their own fury against him because there was no need, since he was destined to die a dreadful death?

He shook away such notions. All woodlands were filled with watching eyes.

For three days he climbed and searched for signs of the great snake Ulukini. Ulukini was there, somewhere, Kotil had said so. But perhaps Bala was not the one meant to discover it. The thought was a happy one. He need not risk death by poison. And yet he went on searching.

And one morning he climbed the highest ridge he had yet come to and looked down into a little saddle in the hills—and there it lay. Ulukini, the last great snake.

He almost cried out in amazement. He had not known it would be so gigantic, lying coiled in a pile taller than a man. Its body was thicker than the bodies of two men and its head was vast.

What he had not known either was that Ulukini was so beautiful. In the morning sun its scales glittered, gold and green and shining blue and purple. The colors moved in waves, the patterns rippled along its back and sides, glowing here, dimming there, but always alive with a cold and vivid fire. Bala caught his breath in his throat. He had not dreamed of such a sight.

For a long time he stared down in wonder. And then he

remembered. He had not come to admire. He had come to make a plan and try to carry it out.

He surveyed the snake and its surroundings carefully. This must be where the monster lived and slept. The ground was worn and bare of vegetation—no trees, no brush, no grass. Several wide paths led away from the spot and into the forest. When Ulukini went in search of food or water—and Bala did not know whether it required food or water, being so nearly immortal—no doubt it followed one of these paths.

In a space he discovered this was true, for the great snake roused itself, weaving its huge head back and forth, unwreathing itself from its heap of gleaming coils, and then sliding lithely off among the trees along one of the paths.

Whether it went for food or drink Bala could not know.

For two days Bala watched the giant snake. He learned about the times of its comings and goings, and that it did not see well but used other senses to guide it, touch and smell and hearing.

Bala went away, for he had made a plan and now must try to carry it out. He killed two animals he did not generally kill, for their flesh was not flavorful, but they were very fat. He scraped the fat carefully into one of the hides he had brought with him, and then he sought something else.

He was fortunate and found it almost at once, quartz stone, that rock which is composed of shining crystals.

He pounded up the rock and added the bright particles to the fat and stirred them together well. He made a sort of bag of the hide and tied the mouth tightly with tough grasses.

Then he returned to Ulukini's lair. He concentrated on each step of his plan and tried to carry it out carefully and not let himself consider failing. Or at any rate not let himself care whether he failed.

One of the great snake's trails sloped away to the west. Bala waited until Ulukini had disappeared along another of its paths, and then he went a short way down the western slope. Using his knife and his hands, he dug a deep and narrow trench. He spent a long time at this task, and when he heard Ulukini returning, the day was nearly over.

Bala went swiftly away and hid himself among the trees and in the darkness polished and sharpened his spear and his knife.

He lay down but he could not sleep. He was afraid to sleep. He was afraid to think lest he think of failing and what would happen to him. He lay and looked up at the forest roof above him and tried to think of nothing at all, and then he fell asleep.

He woke and jumped to his feet, believing he had missed his opportunity. But it was still midnight-dark and he had not slept long.

He spent the time till dawn in misery, turning his mind this way and that, away from the happy past and the strange present and the unknown and foreboding future.

And then the night began to dissolve slowly, trees and bushes became shadows and the spaces between them something lighter than shadow. He let himself think of his plan, going over and over it until he was sure of just what he meant to do and how to do it.

When the light grew strong enough so that he could see plainly, he undid his flask full of fat and quartz and rubbed it carefully over his body. He stood under the trees nearly naked and glistening even in the twilight.

He took his spear and his knife and went softly, softly up the western trail. When he came to the narrow trench he had dug the day before, he stopped. The sun was coming up but was not yet high enough to shine upon him. He waited quietly, taking small, shallow breaths.

He could see above him the shadow of Ulukini coiled asleep at the top of the rise. And then the sun climbed a little higher in the sky and the time had come. The rays fell upon him and he shone like a burning tree. Ulukini would be dazzled, its half-blind eyes would never find this glaring object in the glaring light of daybreak.

Bala shouted, "Ulukini! Oh, giant snake, come here!" He called as loudly as he could and saw the serpent's head raised and the long forked tongue come darting out of the great mouth.

"Come here!" cried Bala. He danced back and forth behind the trench, a brilliant firefly of a man in the red and brilliant light of dawn.

The serpent appeared at the top of the slope, hissing in anger, and the long beautiful body flowed toward him, and Bala's heart beat fast. And still he danced and called.

And when the huge beast was almost upon him, its head almost over the trench, he sprang forward and with all his strength plunged his spear behind the head, between the third and fourth row of scales. In one gesture he freed his weapon and leaped back. He ran far down the slope and stopped and looked up.

He heard the beast utter a long, whispering groan, saw it writhe and slash feebly through the air and then go still.

Was it over then? So quickly and simply? He had truly killed Ulukini, the last great snake? He went slowly back the way he had come and saw that the snake was in fact dying.

The great body quivered faintly and blood gushed from its mouth and from the wound and poured into the trench Bala had dug. The blood smoked and hissed, he could hear it burning down and down into the earth, harmlessly vanishing into the dark depths and rocks.

And while he watched a dreadful thing happened. The colors dimmed along Ulukini's scales, the iridescence faded and went out like the embers of a smoldering fire. The snake was gray and dull and then the body itself began to dwindle and collapse, as a burnt log collapses into ashes.

Within a few minutes nothing remained of the giant snake Ulukini and its marvelous beauty but a twisted ridge of dust. Even the vast head had shrunk and the eyes fallen in and the skull crumbled. Bala could see the shape of the magic stone revealed in the top of the skull.

He could not move. He could only stand and stare. He had thought to do a brave and clever thing and he had merely done a deed full of horror that nothing could undo. Ulukini the last great snake had gone to earth and never again would sunlight or moonlight glisten on those cold rainbow scales. Of all that wonder and loveliness there was now simply this small heap of grime.

After a long while Bala roused himself. He went close to the snake and gazed at the shape of the magic crystal embedded in what was left of the skull. The stone was his by right and yet for a long time he could not make himself reach down and claim it.

Let Ulukini keep it. He would have left it save that he knew someone else would surely find it and he would have done this deed in vain. He took his knife and slid it around the stone—and one tiny last drop of blood flew out and fell upon his forearm.

He was protected by the layer of fat, yet the venom burned into his arm. Frightened, he picked up a handful of dirt and grass and rubbed and rubbed at the spot, but the burning went on.

He was to die then. He had truly killed the snake to no purpose, for now the snake was killing him. He squatted and waited to die, here in this far place by the ruins of mystery and legend.

But he did not die. The burning stopped, and when he looked at his arm, the blood was gone. Only in its place a tiny replica of Ulukini clung to his skin, an infinitesimal snake of green and silver and blue and purple, no bigger than a moth's antenna.

So he would not die, only bear forever the mark of what he had done. He went on with the work he had started and lifted the stone from the skull.

He scarcely dared look at it but carried it away at once into the forest and wrapped it gently in moss and leaves. Then he went back to his sleeping place of the night before and gathered up his few belongings and set out for the valley.

He hurried, for now summer was truly gone and the leaves above his head were beginning to turn color. He had no wish to spend another winter in his house of bones.

He had not left a trail for himself as he had traveled to find Ulukini, but like all good hunters he knew where he was going and how to get there. So it did not take many days before he found himself on the last far slopes of the northern mountains and saw the drying grasses of the valley and the strange bones and then at last his house.

Smoke rose from the hole in the roof and he knew Kotil and Medana had taken over his shelter and he was glad. It was a sign that he should not linger here but travel on at once.

Kotil had sensed his coming and they stood waiting for him.

"We took your house," said Kotil when she had greeted him. "Our second shelter was even weaker than our first and fell of its own weight. We did not know that you would be returning. We are grateful for the use of this one. I will see that it is properly cleansed for you."

Bala shook his head. "It is no matter. The house is yours now. I do not intend to stay here again," he told her.

Kotil looked at him sharply and sadly. "You have done it then?" she asked in a quiet voice.

Bala did not meet her eyes. "I do not know what you mean," he said. He was ashamed of his pretence. Stealthily he touched the little image of the snake on his arm.

"And now you can return," Kotil made a statement rather than a question of the words.

"And now I can return," Bala responded. The three of them stood in silence. Bala thought back over it all, the arrival of the two strangers and Kotil's warning about Medana.

"There is this, Kotil," Bala said at last. "It was not Medana's doing only. The notion was there in my mind all along. Medana merely helped me find it. He could not make me do a thing I knew already I was going to do. It was I who lacked the strength to resist."

"A notion in the mind is one thing," the old woman answered sharply. "Learning how to do a thing and doing it are other things entirely. I should not have stayed here with Medana. But I believed I could protect you."

And Bala remembered how Medana had mocked him and challenged him until Bala could not resist asking Kotil to affirm that Ulukini dwelt in the hills and to tell how it might be killed. He remembered the evening when he and Kotil and Medana had sat around the fire in his house and he, Bala, had been angry and resentful and had let Medana slip into his head the determination to listen to only one of those two people arguing in his mind, the determination to seek out and kill Ulukini.

If he had been strong enough ... if Kotil had taken Medana away ... if Bala had gone away himself ...

"I could not protect you," Kotil said sorrowfully. "It may be that I cannot protect anyone from Medana, but only keep him here, away from everyone, where he can do no further harm."

But Kotil was an old woman. The chain that bound Medana to her would grow weaker. Soon enough he would go back into the world of other people.

Bala looked once again into Medana's eyes. Only death would extinguish the little cold slippery thing that lived in their depths. But because of his nature death would come for Medana sooner than for other young men. What harm he would do he had better do quickly. Soon he would be the victim of his own mischief. He would meet an evil stronger than his own and it would turn on him and kill him.

Bala said nothing of his thoughts. Instead he bade them good-bye and wished them well and began the long walk to his home.

And time went by.

The journey back took much more time than it had taken Bala to reach the valley of strange bones. The weather turned cold and there was often rain or even snow. And Bala had now in his keeping a magic crystal, so he traveled always away from paths and trails. He did not know whom he might meet who could discern the stone's presence and try to take it away from him.

And he went with care in order not to offend the stone and gave it frequently water from the clearest springs he could find and sometimes a drop or two of deer's blood. He did not know how properly such things were done, but he did them as well as he could and asked the stone over and over to forgive him for his clumsiness and ignorance.

In its nest of moss and leaves the stone continued to glow and flash and he assumed that it was pleased.

It was good that he had the stone to tend, for the slowness of his journey pricked him and made him impatient, and he could not keep himself from thinking of his wife and children and the chance that he might once more be with them. Only the care of the stone kept his mind from such thoughts.

And at last he was among hills and streams he recognized and he went more swiftly, though still keeping himself hidden. And on the day he reached his village it was almost dark and he waited, sleepless, till morning before he entered the town.

He waited till the day was well begun and most of the people gathered in the market place. He walked then openly and firmly into their midst. He went straight to Gatani and put into the other man's hands the moss within which lay the shining crystal.

"I have brought you a magic stone," said Bala. "To replace the one you have lost."

Gatani stared at Bala and then looked down into his hands. Carefully, with his thumb, he brushed away the moss until the stone glowed forth. Gatani sprang to his feet.

"So!" he cried scornfully. "You have grown weary of

exile and have returned my magic stone to me! You have brought back my magic stone!"

Bala could not speak. That he should have done and endured all that he had done and endured and have it come to this: That Gatani should still accuse him of theft and dishonor.

He staggered as if from a blow and from shock he could not speak. He heard sounds of disapproval from those around him and saw their hostile looks, but in a kind of daze.

He raised his hand and caught Gatani's arm and steadied himself and found his voice.

"This is not your stone!" he shouted and heard how fierce, how hoarse with fury was the sound of his own words. "To get this stone I killed the last great serpent, Ulukini. I give it to you freely, to replace your stone. But it was I who killed the snake and I who bear the mark of its death."

He extended his forearm and pointed to the tiny snake there.

Gatani leaned forward. "I see no mark," he said at last. And he called for two elders of the village, who served as priests, to come forward and look.

"We see no mark," they repeated. "Besides it is not possible that the last great serpent is dead."

Bala touched the little snake wonderingly. Was it true? Could no one see the brand except himself? He should not have concealed it from Kotil. She perhaps might have seen it or told him why it would be hidden from others.

And now he stood among those who had once been his friends, and considered that he had done a dreadful thing for no reason at all. He was not to regain the love of his family or the respect of his townsmen.

He raised his eyes to Gatani's.

"Ask the stone," he said furiously. "I dare you to ask the stone itself whether I robbed you of your magic crystal and whether this is it."

Gatani frowned. He was afraid of the stone and of asking it questions. Yet he could not refuse what Bala asked and he knew it.

"It will take two days," he said after a while.

"I have been gone nearly two years," Bala replied. "I can wait another two days."

"Very well," agreed Gatani. He went away carrying the stone and the elders went with him to see that all was done properly.

Bala's wife came to his side and put her hand on his arm and he went with her to their house. And for those two days she did not leave him to work in her garden or go to the market place.

They said little to each other of the nearly two years which were gone and could not be recalled, for there was little to say. Bala's children had grown so that he scarcely recognized them and they did not remember him. Yet he saw no way to change things and spoke to them as a father would and held them in his arms.

Bala's wife said she saw the tiny snake on his forearm, but when he asked her to touch it, she put her finger on the wrong spot and he knew she had lied to comfort him, because she loved him.

And the two days came to an end. Gatani came into the market place with the elders and stood before all the people.

In two days Gatani had grown old, for it is a trying and dangerous thing to look into the depths of a magic crystal and see the truth. The truth may crack a heart.

Gatani spoke and everyone listened with care.

"This magic stone is not my magic stone," he said. "Bala did not steal my stone. My stone grew angry with me, so angry that it swallowed itself. I do not know how I offended it. Perhaps I gave it too much deer's blood or too little. Or perhaps there was something I should have done and failed to do without knowing. Whatever happened, Bala did not take my stone and I accused him wrongly. This is the magic crystal from the head of the last giant snake, Ulukini."

A man called out, "Ah, you are not worthy to own the stone and look into its depths!"

And many people nodded and looked coldly at Gatani. And Bala stepped up beside him and motioned that he had something to say and everyone listened.

"Once I was a man of honor and I lived in this village," he said. "I have been away for nearly two years. Now I am come home and am once again a man of honor. I did not come home in order that another man should go away and take my place in loneliness and disgrace. Gatani was in error, but he acted as he thought he must. He did not then know the truth. I have brought him another stone. It is his and he must decide whether it shall take the place of the one given him by his grandfather."

"This is so," said one of the elders. "What Bala has said is right and as it should be."

And Gatani took his place again in the market and was treated as he had always been. But everyone saw that Gatani had changed. For though he knew he would never be an elder or a great hunter or storyteller or maker of spears, yet he had always walked with pride because his grandfather had chosen him to receive the magic stone. Now he walked with bent head and seldom spoke and was older than his years.

And what became of the stone from the head of Ulukini no one knew except the elders, and they did not say.

So once more Bala lived in his house with his wife and his children and he spoke to them as a husband and father would. He taught his children songs and games and told them what was right to do. He hunted for meat and skins. His wife worked in her garden and helped Bala prepare the skins for sale in the market. Bala traded in the market and everyone came to trade with him and tell him where the hunting was good and who had a new baby and that a wolf had been seen near the town, and news of such sort.

And Bala was again a man of honor and happy to be once more at home with his family and friends.

Yet sometimes he went into the forest and sat alone and touched the tiny snake on his arm, that only he could see. He thought about honor and what it was and what it was worth. He thought of Kotil and Medana, and of Gatani.

But most of all he thought about Ulukini, the last great snake, and of its beauty and how its colors had once glistened in the sun and now would glisten no more.

And time went by.

Interpretive Questions

1. Why is Bala, a hunter, at war with himself over the idea of seeking out and killing Ulukini? (25-26)

2. Why does Kotil insist that, without Medana, Bala would never have killed the last great snake? (38)

3. Is the story suggesting that human beings are better off not having access to "true things"?

Thinking Interpretively: Theme

Every story presents us with distinctive characters in a unique situation and setting. Even when we are not given every single detail about the characters and their lives, we can still describe what a particular story is "about." We do not know exactly where or when "The Last Great Snake" takes place, but we can say that it concerns a hunter named Bala, who is wrongly accused of stealing a magic stone and exiles himself from his community as a result. To regain his honor among his people, he decides to replace the lost stone, but in order to do so, he has to destroy Ulukini, the last of seven beautiful, "nearly immortal" great snakes.

A statement like this tells us what happens in "The Last Great Snake." But when we start thinking interpretively about a story, we also want to explore its *theme* or *themes*—what the story is "about" in more general, universal terms. For example, even in our brief summary of what happens in "The Last Great Snake," we find hints that the story may have something to say about honor, or belonging to a community, or making a difficult decision. These are ideas we all can understand, even if we did not grow up in a culture like Bala's and never expect to meet a giant snake. Themes are like bridges between our lives and the lives in the story, enabling us to enter into and learn from situations quite unlike our own.

Different readers will have different things to say about a story's theme. This is not surprising, since the individual experiences and values that each reader brings to a story influence which details he or she finds most significant. And it is these details that shape a reader's views about the basic issues of a story. One reader, for instance, might see man's destruction of nature's beauty as the key issue of "The Last Great Snake," while another might say that the main theme is the human need for companionship.

How do we define for ourselves the theme or themes of a story? And how can exploring a theme help us to interpret a story?

We can begin by reflecting on those parts of a story that we find most intriguing or puzzling or that create the greatest uneasiness in us. For example, after reading "The Last Great Snake," we wondered why Bala didn't defend his honor by telling the villagers the truth about why he entered Gatani's house. In order to answer this question, we found that we needed to look more closely at the way the ideas of "truth" and "honor" are treated in the story. This led us to further questions. For example, *Why are the villagers so afraid of the truth-telling stone, believing that "the truth might crack a heart or make a brain go numb forever"? Why does Bala think of himself as "a man without honor," even though he knows he did not steal the stone?* Finally, *Why can truth and honor, which are both good things, be obtained only by killing Ulukini, which is presented as a temptation to do evil?*

Our consideration of the themes of truth and honor thus brings us to yet another theme—the conflict between good and evil. *Is the story saying that Bala should have resisted the temptation to kill Ulukini, and so sacrificed his claim to truth and honor? Or is it saying that in this world good is always mixed with evil?* As we think interpretively about the theme of good versus evil in "The Last Great Snake," we find ourselves seeking help from the details of the story: *What is the invisible "chain" binding the tempter Medana and the good Kotil? Why are we told that the chain will grow weaker? Why are both Medana and Bala represented as excellent hunters and sometimes as rivals?*

Thinking about theme sends us back again and again to the details of the story. Imagine this process—one of moving back and forth between asking and answering questions about a story's details and about its broader issues or themes—as a kind of conversation with yourself that will take you ever deeper into the story's meaning. The longer your internal conversation continues, the more you will understand the story and appreciate the way all its elements—character, plot, symbol, the world of the story—work together. ▮▮

The Secret Lion

Alberto Alvaro Rios

I was twelve and in junior high school and something happened that we didn't have a name for, but it was there nonetheless like a lion, and roaring, roaring that way the biggest things do. Everything changed. Just that. Like the rug, the one that gets pulled—or better, like the tablecloth those magicians pull where the stuff on the table stays the same but the gasp! from the audience makes the staying-the-same part not matter. Like that.

What happened was there were teachers now, not just one teacher, teach-erz, and we felt personally abandoned somehow. When a person had all these teachers now, he didn't get taken care of the same way, even though six was more than one. Arithmetic went out the door when we walked in. And we saw girls now, but they weren't the same girls we used to know because we couldn't talk to them anymore, not the same way we used to, certainly not to

Sandy, even though she was my neighbor, too. Not even to her. She just played the piano all the time. And there were words, oh there were words in junior high school, and we wanted to know what they were, and how a person did them—that's what school was supposed to be for. Only, in junior high school, school wasn't school, everything was backward-like. If you went up to a teacher and said the word to try and find out what it meant you got in trouble for saying it. So we didn't. And we figured it must have been that way about other stuff, too, so we never said anything about anything—we weren't stupid.

But my friend Sergio and I, we solved junior high school. We would come home from school on the bus, put our books away, change shoes, and go across the highway to the arroyo. It was the one place we were not supposed to go. So we did. This was, after all, what junior high had at least shown us. It was our river, though, our personal Mississippi, our friend from long back, and it was full of stories and all the branch forts we had built in it when we were still the Vikings of America, with our own symbol, which we had carved everywhere, even in the sand, which let the water take it. That was good, we had decided; whoever was at the end of this river would know about us.

At the very very top of our growing lungs, what we would do down there was shout every dirty word we could think of, in every combination we could come up with, and we would yell about girls, and all the things we wanted to do with them, as loud as we could—we didn't know what we wanted to do with them, just things—and we would yell about teachers, and how we loved some of them, like Miss Crevelone, and how we wanted to dissect some of them, making signs of the cross, like priests, and we would yell this stuff over and over because it felt good, we couldn't explain why, it just felt good and for the first time in our lives there was nobody to tell us we couldn't. So we did.

One Thursday we were walking along shouting this way, and the railroad, the Southern Pacific, which ran above and along the far side of the arroyo, had dropped a grinding ball down there, which was, we found out later, a cannonball thing used in mining. A bunch of them were put in a big vat which turned around and crushed the ore. One had been dropped, or thrown—what do caboose men do when they get bored—but it got down there regardless and as we were walking along yelling about one girl or another, a particular Claudia, we found it, one of these things, looked at it, picked it up, and got very excited, and held it and passed it back and forth, and we were saying "Guythisis, this is, geeGuythis . . . ": we had this perception about nature then, that nature is imperfect and that round things are perfect: we said "GuyGodthis is perfect, thisisthis is perfect, it's round, round and heavy, it'sit's the best thing we'veeverseen. Whatisit?" We didn't know. We just knew it was great. We just, whatever, we played with it, held it some more.

And then we had to decide what to do with it. We knew, because of a lot of things, that if we were going to take this and show it to anybody, this discovery, this best thing, was going to be taken away from us. That's the way it works with little kids, like all the polished quartz, the tons of it we had collected piece by piece over the years. Junior high kids too. If we took it home, my mother, we knew, was going to look at it and say "throw that dirty thing in the, get rid of it." Simple like, like that. "But ma it's the best thing I" "Getridofit." Simple.

So we didn't. Take it home. Instead, we came up with the answer. We dug a hole and we buried it. And we marked it secretly. Lots of secret signs. And came back the next week to dig it up and, we didn't know, pass it around some more or something, but we didn't find it. We dug up that whole bank, and we never found it again. We tried.

Sergio and I talked about that ball or whatever it was when we couldn't find it. All we used were small words, neat, good. Kid words. What we were really saying, but didn't know the words, was how much that ball was like that place, that whole arroyo: couldn't tell anybody about it, didn't understand what it was, didn't have a name for it. It just felt good. It was just perfect in the way it was that place, that whole going to that place, that whole junior high school lion. It was just iron-heavy, it had no name, it felt good or not, we couldn't take it home to show our mothers, and once we buried it, it was gone forever.

The ball was gone, like the first reasons we had come to that arroyo years earlier, like the first time we had seen the arroyo, it was gone like everything else that had been taken away. This was not our first lesson. We stopped going to the arroyo after not finding the thing, the same way we had stopped going there years earlier and headed for the mountains. Nature seemed to keep pushing us around one way or another, teaching us the same thing every place we ended up. Nature's gang was tough that way, teaching us stuff.

When we were young we moved away from town, me and my family. Sergio's was already out there. Out in the wilds. Or at least the new place seemed like the wilds since everything looks bigger the smaller a man is. I was five, I guess, and we had moved three miles north of Nogales where we had lived, three miles north of the Mexican border. We looked across the highway in one direction and there was the arroyo; hills stood up in the other direction. Mountains, for a small man.

When the first summer came the very first place we went to was of course the one place we weren't supposed to go, the arroyo. We went down in there and found water running, summer rain water mostly, and we went swimming. But every third or fourth or fifth day, the sewage treatment plant that was, we found out, upstream, would release whatever it was that it released, and we would never know exactly what day that was, and a person really couldn't tell right off by looking at the water, not every time, not so a person could get out in time. So, we went swimming that summer and some days we had a lot of fun. Some days we didn't. We found a thousand ways to explain what happened on those other days, constructing elaborate stories about the neighborhood dogs, and hadn't she, my mother, miscalculated her step before, too? But she knew something was up because we'd come running into the house those days, wanting to take a shower, even—if this can be imagined—in the middle of the day.

That was the first time we stopped going to the arroyo. It taught us to look the other way. We decided, as the second side of summer came, we wanted to go into the mountains. They were still mountains then. We went running in one summer Thursday morning, my friend Sergio and I, into my mother's kitchen, and said, well, what'zin, what'zin those hills over there—we used her word so she'd understand us—and she said nothingdon'tworryaboutit. So we went out, and we weren't dumb, we thought with our eyes to each other, ohhoshe'stryingtokeepsomething-fromus. We knew adults.

We had read the books, after all; we knew about bridges and castles and wildtreacherousraging alligatormouth rivers. We wanted them. So we were going to go out and get them. We went back that morning into that kitchen and we said "We're going out there, we're going into the hills, we're going away for three days, don't worry." She said, "All right."

"You know," I said to Sergio, "if we're going to go away for three days, well, we ought to at least pack a lunch."

But we were two young boys with no patience for what we thought at the time was mom-stuff: making sa-and-wiches. My mother didn't offer. So we got out little kid knapsacks that my mother had sewn for us, and into them we put the jar of mustard. A loaf of bread. Knivesforks-plates, bottles of Coke, a can opener. This was lunch for the two of us. And we were weighed down, humped over to be strong enough to carry this stuff. But we started walking anyway, into the hills. We were going to eat berries and stuff otherwise. "Goodbye." My mom said that.

After the first hill we were dead. But we walked. My mother could still see us. And we kept walking. We walked until we got to where the sun is straight overhead, noon. That place. Where that is doesn't matter; it's time to eat. The truth is we weren't anywhere close to that place. We just agreed that the sun was overhead and that it was time to eat, and by tilting our heads a little we could make that the truth.

"We really ought to start looking for a place to eat."

"Yeah. Let's look for a good place to eat." We went back and forth saying that for fifteen minutes, making it lunchtime because that's what we always said back and forth before lunchtimes at home. "Yeah, I'm hungry all right." I nodded my head. "Yeah, I'm hungry all right too. I'm hungry." He nodded his head. I nodded my head back. After a good deal more nodding, we were ready, just as we came over a little hill. We hadn't found the mountains yet. This was a little hill.

And on the other side of this hill we found heaven.

It was just what we thought it would be.

Perfect. Heaven was green, like nothing else in Arizona. And it wasn't a cemetery or like that because we had seen cemeteries and they had gravestones and stuff and this didn't. This was perfect, had trees, lots of trees, had birds, like we had never seen before. It was like "The Wizard of Oz," like when they got to Oz and everything was so green, so emerald, they had to wear those glasses, and we ran just like them, laughing, laughing that way we did that moment, and we went running down to this clearing in it all, hitting each other that good way we did.

We got down there, we kept laughing, we kept hitting each other, we unpacked our stuff, and we started acting "rich." We knew all about how to do that, like blowing on our nails, then rubbing them on our chests for the shine. We made our sandwiches, opened our Cokes, got out the rest of the stuff, the salt and pepper shakers. I found this particular hole and I put my Coke right into it, a perfect fit, and I called it my Coke-holder. I got down next to it on my back, because everyone knows that rich people eat lying down, and I got my sandwich in one hand and put my other arm around the Coke in its holder. When I wanted a drink, I lifted my neck a little, put out my lips, and tipped my Coke a little with the crook of my elbow. Ah.

We were there, lying down, eating our sandwiches, laughing, throwing bread at each other and out for the birds. This was heaven. We were laughing and we couldn't believe it. My mother *was* keeping something from us, ah ha, but we had found her out. We even found water over at the side of the clearing to wash our plates with—we had brought plates. Sergio started washing his plates when he was done, and I was being rich with my Coke, and this day in summer was right.

When suddenly these two men came, from around a corner of trees and the tallest grass we had ever seen. They had bags on their backs, leather bags, bags and sticks.

We didn't know what clubs were, but I learned later, like I learned about the grinding balls. The two men yelled at us. Most specifically, one wanted me to take my Coke out of my Coke-holder so he could sink his golf ball into it.

Something got taken away from us that moment. Heaven. We grew up a little bit, and couldn't go backward. We learned. No one had ever told us about golf. They had told us about heaven. And it went away. We got golf in exchange.

We went back to the arroyo for the rest of that summer, and tried to have fun the best we could. We learned to be ready for finding the grinding ball. We loved it, and when we buried it we knew what would happen. The truth is, we didn't look so hard for it. We were two boys and twelve summers then, and not stupid. Things get taken away.

We buried it because it was perfect. We didn't tell my mother, but together it was all we talked about, till we forgot. It was the lion.

Interpretive Questions

1. Why do the boys go to the arroyo to solve their junior high school problems? (51-52)

2. Why does the narrator say that the grinding ball "was the lion," and that once it was buried "it was gone forever"? (53, 58)

3. Why does the loss of "heaven" on the golf course make the boys "ready for finding the grinding ball" when they are older? (58)

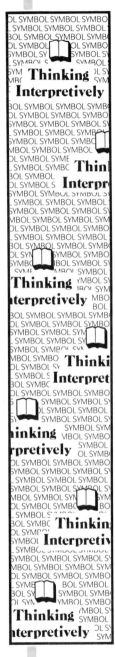

Thinking Interpretively: Symbol

In everyday life, we constantly use symbols—that is, signs or objects that stand for something else. Some symbols are "public" in the sense that they carry the same associations for everyone: a skull and crossbones, for example, traditionally communicates danger and death. When used by writers, however, such symbols often take on additional shades of meaning. For instance, in "The Last Great Snake," the hero Bala, who has been cast out of his community, lives for a time in a hut built of bones—an image suggesting that without other people, he is like a dead person. Writers may also create their own personal symbols. These "private" symbols do not ask us to fix on a single exact meaning; rather, they suggest a broad range of feeling and ideas. For this reason, although they may at first be more puzzling for the reader, they can also prove to be the richest and most satisfying kind of symbol.

Private symbols are at the very heart of "The Secret Lion." In this story, the narrator talks about his feelings in junior high school, a time when "everything changed." Because he can't express to himself what he is experiencing—because his complex feelings are so new to him—he tries to explain the experience through symbols like the arroyo, the grinding ball, and the roaring lion. In order to fully understand the story, we have to enter into the narrator's personal, private symbols and try to figure out what they mean to him and why they are so important.

One way for you to enter into these private symbols is to think about how they are connected with your own experience. For example, do you have a place that you keep going back to? Where you can really be yourself, think about things, talk with your friends, and even act crazy? In thinking about your place, you can begin to share the narrator's feelings about the arroyo, and so better understand how going there helps him solve his junior high school problems.

Another important symbol in "The Secret Lion" is the mysterious grinding ball, an object that the boys find "perfect" in its roundness and heaviness. In order to understand why the boys are so interested in the ball, we found it helpful to think about what ideas or feelings they might associate with it. *What is it about the ball's heaviness that appeals to the boys? Does it appear to them as a kind of anchor during this period of change and upset? Does possessing the "iron-heavy" ball give them a sense of their own secret power or strength?* Thinking about its qualities in this way helped us to interpret what the boys do with the grinding ball, and answer such questions as *Why do the boys bury the ball? Why do they mark the spot with "lots of secret signs"? Why do they keep the grinding ball a secret even after they have hidden it?*

In addition to exploring a particular symbol, we can also consider how the various symbols in a story work together. For example, we noticed that the boys' ritual of burying the ball in the arroyo is like their childhood games when they were "Vikings of America" and carved their sign everywhere. In both instances, the boys are enjoying creating an atmosphere of mystery, power, and control. Getting closer to the boys' state of mind in this way can prepare us to consider such issues as why they stop going to the arroyo after they lose the grinding ball, and how both the arroyo and the ball contribute to their sense that "things get taken away." And so, in the process of coming to our own understanding of the author's private symbols, we grasp more fully the meaning of the story as a whole.

As you read "The Secret Lion" for the second time, try to figure out why the narrator thinks of junior high as being like a lion. What words or ideas do you associate with lions? Why does burying the grinding ball in the arroyo—hiding a "perfect" thing in their own private place—make the boys feel better about "the lion"? ▮▮

CHARACTERS IN "THE JUNGLE BOOKS"

(pronunciations based on the Hindi)

AKELA [A-*kay*-la] The leader of the Seeonee wolf pack when Mowgli comes to the jungle as a baby; also called the Lone Wolf.

BAGHEERA [Bag-eera, pronounced like an "era" in history] The black panther who, for the price of a newly slain bull, bought the infant Mowgli's acceptance into the Seeonee wolf pack.

BALOO [*Bar*-loo] The wise, old brown bear who teaches wolf cubs the Law of the Jungle. He, along with Bagheera, spoke in favor of admitting Mowgli into the Seeonee wolf pack.

BANDAR-LOG [Bunder-logue] The Monkey-people.

BULDEO [*Bul*-doo] The village hunter who led the movement to cast Mowgli out.

CHIL [Cheel] The kite, a bird of prey and a scavenger.

DHOLE [Dole] A fierce, wild red dog of India.

FERAO [Feer-*ow*] The scarlet woodpecker.

HATHI [Huttee] The elephant, also called the Silent One.

KAA [Kar, with a sort of gasp in it] The rock python who befriends Mowgli; head of the Middle Jungle.

MESSUA [*Mes*-war] Mowgli's human mother.

MOWGLI ["Mow" rhymes with "cow"] The boy who grows up as a wolf in the jungles of India.

MYSA [*Mi*-sar] The wild buffalo.

NATHOO [Nut-too] Messua's name for Mowgli.

RAKSHA [*Ruck*sher] "The Demon"—Mowgli's wolf mother. Her children, including Grey Brother, are known as the Four.

SEEONEE [See-*own*-y] The name of Mowgli's wolf pack.

SHERE KHAN [Sheer Karn] The tiger who hunted Mowgli and whom Mowgli eventually slays; also called Lungri, the Lame One.

TABAQUI [Ta-*bar*-kee] The jackal, a follower of Shere Khan; also called Dish-licker.

The Jungle Books

Rudyard Kipling

Letting in the Jungle

You will remember, if you have read the tales in the first *Jungle Book,* that after Mowgli had pinned Shere Khan's hide to the Council Rock, he told as many as were left of the Seeonee Pack that henceforward he would hunt in the jungle alone; and the four children of Mother and Father Wolf said that they would hunt with him. But it is not easy to change all one's life at once—particularly in the jungle. The first thing Mowgli did, when the disorderly pack had slunk off, was to go to the home-cave, and sleep for a day and a night. Then he told Mother Wolf and Father Wolf as much as they could understand of his adventures among men. And when he made the morning sun flicker up and down the blade of his skinning-knife—the same he had skinned Shere Khan with—they said he had learnt something. Then Akela and Grey Brother had to explain their share of the great buffalo-drive in the ravine,* and Baloo toiled up the hill to hear all about it, and Bagheera scratched himself all over with pure delight at the way in which Mowgli had managed his war.

It was long after sunrise, but no one dreamed of going to sleep, and from time to time, Mother Wolf would throw up her head, and sniff a deep snuff of satisfaction as the wind brought her the smell of the tiger-skin on the Council Rock.

"But for Akela and Grey Brother here," Mowgli said, at the end, "I could have done nothing. Oh, Mother, Mother! If thou hadst seen the blue herd-bulls pour down the ravine, or hurry through the gates when the man pack flung stones at me!"

"I am glad I did not see that last," said Mother Wolf, stiffly. "It is not *my* custom to suffer my cubs to be driven to and fro like jackals! *I* would have taken a price from the man pack, but I would have spared the woman who gave thee the milk. Yes, I would have spared her alone."

"Peace, peace, Raksha!" said Father Wolf, lazily. "Our frog has come back again—so wise that his own father must lick his feet. And what is a cut, more or less, on the head? Leave Man alone." Baloo and Bagheera both echoed: "Leave Man alone."

Mowgli, his head on Mother Wolf's side, smiled con-

---

*In "Tiger-Tiger!" Mowgli kills his enemy Shere Khan by trapping the tiger in a ravine through which he drives a herd of buffalo. When the villagers, fearing this "magic," throw stones at Mowgli, he angrily turns the herd and drives it through the village.

tentedly, and said that, for his own part, he never wished to see, or hear, or smell Man again.

"But what," said Akela, cocking one ear, "but what if men do not leave thee alone, Little Brother?"

"We be *five*," said Grey Brother, looking round at the company, and snapping his jaws on the last word.

"We also might attend to that hunting," said Bagheera, with a little *switch-switch* of his tail, looking at Baloo. "But why think of Man now, Akela?"

"For this reason," the Lone Wolf answered. "When that yellow thief's hide was hung up on the rock, I went back along our trail to the village, stepping in my tracks, turning aside, and lying down, to make a mixed trail in case any should follow us. But when I had fouled the trail so that I myself hardly knew it again, Mang the Bat came hawking between the trees, and hung up above me. Said Mang: 'The village of the man pack, where they cast out the man-cub, hums like a hornet's nest.' "

"It was a big stone that I threw," chuckled Mowgli, who had often amused himself by throwing ripe pawpaws into a hornet's nest, and racing to the nearest pool before the hornets caught him.

"I asked of Mang what he had seen. He said that the Red Flower blossomed at the gate of the village, and men sat about it carrying guns. Now *I* know, for I have good cause"—Akela looked here at the old dry scars on his flank and side—"that men do not carry guns for pleasure. Presently, Little Brother, a man with a gun follows our trail—if, indeed, he be not already on it."

"But why should he? Men have cast me out. What more do they need?" said Mowgli angrily.

"Thou art a man, Little Brother," Akela returned. "It is not for us, the Free Hunters, to tell thee what thy brethren do, or why."

He had just time to snatch up his paw as the skinning-knife cut deep into the ground below. Mowgli struck quicker than an average human eye could follow, but Akela was a wolf, and even a dog, who is very far removed from the wild wolf, his ancestor, can be waked out of deep sleep by a cart-wheel touching his flank, and can spring away unharmed before that wheel comes on.

"Another time," Mowgli said, quietly, returning the knife to its sheath, "speak of the man pack and of Mowgli in *two* breaths—not one."

"*Phff!* That is a sharp tooth," said Akela, snuffing at the blade's cut in the earth, "but living with the man pack has spoiled thine eye, Little Brother. I could have killed buck while thou was striking."

Bagheera sprang to his feet, thrust up his head as far as he could, sniffed, and stiffened through every curve in his body. Grey Brother followed his example quickly, keeping a little to his left to get the wind that was blowing from the right, while Akela bounded fifty yards upwind, and, half-crouching, stiffened too. Mowgli looked on enviously. He could smell things as very few human beings could, but he had never reached the hair-trigger-like sensitiveness of a jungle nose, and his three months in the smoky village had put him back sadly. However, he dampened his finger, rubbed it on his nose, and stood erect to catch the upper scent, which, though the faintest, is the truest.

"Man!" Akela growled, dropping on his haunches.

"Buldeo!" said Mowgli, sitting down. "He follows our trail, and yonder is the sunlight on his gun. Look!"

It was no more than a splash of sunlight, for a fraction of a second, on the brass clamps of the old Tower musket, but nothing in the jungle winks with just that flash, except when the clouds race over the sky. Then a piece of mica, or a little pool, or even a highly polished leaf will flash like a heliograph. But that day was cloudless and still.

"I knew men would follow," said Akela, triumphantly. "Not for nothing have I led the pack!"

Mowgli's four wolves said nothing, but ran down hill on their bellies, melting into the thorn and underbrush.

"Whither go ye, and without word?" Mowgli called.

"*Hsh!* We roll his skull here before midday!" Grey Brother answered.

"Back! Back and wait! Man does not eat Man!" Mowgli shrieked.

"Who was a wolf but now? Who drove the knife at me for thinking he might be a man?" said Akela, as the Four turned back sullenly and dropped to heel.

"Am I to give reason for all I choose to do?" said Mowgli, furiously.

"That is Man! There speaks Man!" Bagheera muttered under his whiskers. "Even so did men talk round the king's cages at Oodeypore. We of the jungle know that Man is wisest of all. If we trusted our ears we should know that of all things he is most foolish." Raising his voice, he added: "The man-cub is right in this. Men hunt in packs. To kill one, unless we know what the others will do, is bad hunting. Come, let us see what this man means towards us."

"We will not come," Grey Brother growled. "Hunt alone, Little Brother. *We* know our own minds! The skull would have been ready to bring by now."

Mowgli had been looking from one to the other of his friends, his chest heaving and his eyes full of tears. He strode forward, and, dropping on one knee, said: "Do I not know my mind? Look at me!"

They looked uneasily, and when their eyes wandered, he called them back again and again, till their hair stood up all over their bodies, and they trembled in every limb, while Mowgli stared and stared.

"Now," said he, "of us five, which is leader?"

"Thou art leader, Little Brother," said Grey Brother, and he licked Mowgli's foot.

"Follow, then," said Mowgli, and the Four followed at his heels with their tails between their legs.

"This comes of living with the man pack," said Bagheera, slipping down after them. "There is more in the jungle now than Jungle Law, Baloo."

The old bear said nothing, but he thought many things.

Mowgli cut across noiselessly through the jungle, at right angles to Buldeo's path, till, parting the undergrowth, he saw the old man, his musket on his shoulder, running up the two-day-old trail at a dog-trot.

You will remember that Mowgli had left the village with

the heavy weight of Shere Khan's raw hide on his shoulders, while Akela and Grey Brother trotted behind, so that the trail was very clearly marked. Presently Buldeo came to where Akela, as you know, had gone back and mixed it all up. Then he sat down, and coughed and grunted, and made little casts round about into the jungle to pick it up again, and all the time he could have thrown a stone over those who were watching him. No one can be so silent as a wolf when he does not care to be heard, and Mowgli, though the wolves thought he moved very clumsily, could come and go like a shadow. They ringed the old man as a school of porpoises ring a steamer at full speed, and as they ringed him they talked unconcernedly, for their speech began below the lowest end of the scale that untaught human beings can hear. (The other end is bounded by the high squeak of Mang the Bat, which very many people cannot catch at all. From that note all the bird and bat and insect talk takes on.)

"This is better than any kill," said Grey Brother, as Buldeo stooped and peered and puffed. "He looks like a lost pig in the jungles by the river. What does he say?" Buldeo was muttering savagely.

Mowgli translated. "He says that packs of wolves must have danced round me. He says that he never saw such a trail in his life. He says he is tired."

"He will be rested before he picks it up again," said Bagheera coolly, as he slipped round a tree-trunk, in the game of blind-man's-buff that they were playing. "*Now,* what does the lean thing do?"

"Eat or blow smoke out of his mouth. Men always play with their mouths," said Mowgli. And the silent trailers saw the old man fill and light, and puff at a water-pipe, and they took good note of the smell of the tobacco, so as to be sure of Buldeo in the darkest night, if necessary.

Then a little knot of charcoal-burners came down the path, and naturally halted to speak to Buldeo, whose fame as a hunter reached for at least twenty miles round. They all sat down and smoked, and Bagheera and the others came up and watched while Buldeo began to tell the story of Mowgli the Devil-Child from one end to another, with additions and inventions. How he himself had really killed Shere Khan; and how Mowgli had turned himself into a wolf, and fought with him all the afternoon, and changed into a boy again and bewitched Buldeo's rifle, so that the bullet turned the corner, when he pointed it at Mowgli, and killed one of Buldeo's own buffaloes; and how the village, knowing him to be the bravest hunter in Seeonee, had sent him out to kill this devil-child. But meantime the village had got hold of Messua and her husband, who were undoubtedly the father and mother of this devil-child, and had barricaded them in their own hut, and presently would torture them to make them confess they were witch and wizard, and then they would be burned to death.

"When?" said the charcoal-burners, because they would very much like to be present at the ceremony.

Buldeo said that nothing would be done till he returned, because the village wished him to kill the jungle boy first. After that they would dispose of Messua and her husband, and divide their land and buffaloes among the village.

Messua's husband had some remarkably fine buffaloes, too. It was an excellent thing to destroy wizards, Buldeo thought, and people who entertained wolf-children out of the jungle were clearly the worst kind of witches.

But, said the charcoal-burners, what would happen if the English heard of it? The English, they had been told, were a perfectly mad people, who would not let honest farmers kill witches in peace.

Why, said Buldeo, the head-man of the village would report that Messua and her husband had died of snakebite. That was all arranged, and the only thing now was to kill the wolf-child. They did not happen to have seen anything of such a creature?

The charcoal-burners looked round cautiously, and thanked their stars they had not, but they had no doubt that so brave a man as Buldeo would find him if any one could. The sun was getting rather low, and they had an idea that they would push on to Buldeo's village and see the wicked witch. Buldeo said that, though it was his duty to kill the devil-child he could not think of letting a party of unarmed men go through the jungle, which might reveal the wolf-demon at any minute, without his escort. He, therefore, would accompany them, and if the sorcerer's child appeared—well, he would show them how the best hunter in Seeonee dealt with such things. The Brahmin, he said, had given him a charm against the creature that made everything perfectly safe.

"What says he? What says he? What says he?" the wolves repeated every few minutes. And Mowgli translated until he came to the witch part of the story, which was a little beyond him, and then he said that the man and woman who had been so kind to him were trapped.

"Do men trap men?" said Grey Brother.

"So he says. I cannot understand the talk. They are all mad together. What have Messua and her man to do with me that they should be put in a trap, and what is all this talk about the Red Flower? I must look to this. Whatever they would do to Messua they will not do till Buldeo returns. And so—" Mowgli thought hard with his fingers playing round the haft of his skinning-knife, while Buldeo and the charcoal-burners went off very valiantly in single file.

"I go hot-foot back to the man pack," Mowgli said at last.

"And those?" said Grey Brother, looking hungrily after the brown backs of the charcoal-burners.

"Sing them home," said Mowgli with a grin. "I do not wish them to be at the village gate till it is dark. Can ye hold them?"

Grey Brother bared his white teeth in contempt. "We can head them round and round in circles like tethered goats—if I know Man."

"That I do not need. Sing to them a little lest they be lonely on the road, and, Grey Brother, the song need not be of the sweetest. Go with them, Bagheera, and help make that song. When night is laid down, meet me by the village—Grey Brother knows the place."

"It is no light hunting to track for a man-cub. When shall I sleep?" said Bagheera, yawning, though his eyes showed he was delighted with the amusement. "Me to sing to naked men! But let us try."

He lowered his head so that the sound would travel, and cried a long, long "Good hunting"—a midnight call in the afternoon, which was quite awful enough to begin with. Mowgli heard it rumble, and rise, and fall, and die off in a creepy sort of whine behind him, and laughed to himself as he ran through the jungle. He could see the charcoal-burners huddled in a knot, old Buldeo's gun-barrel waving, like a banana-leaf, to every point of the compass at once. Then Grey Brother gave the *Ya-la-hi! Yalaha!* call for the buck-driving, when the pack drives the nilghai, the big blue cow, before them, and it seemed to come from the very ends of the earth, nearer, and nearer, and nearer, till it ended in a shriek snapped off short. The other three answered, till even Mowgli could have vowed that the full pack was in full cry, and then they all broke into the magnificent morning-song in the jungle, with every turn, and flourish, and grace-note, that a deep-mouthed wolf of the pack knows. This is a rough rendering of the song, but you must imagine what it sounds like when it breaks the afternoon hush of the jungle:

> One moment past our bodies cast
> > No shadow on the plain;
> Now clear and black they stride our track,
> > And we run home again.
> In morning-hush, each rock and bush
> > Stands hard, and high, and raw:
> Then give the call: *"Good rest to all*
> > *That keep the Jungle Law!"*

Now horn and pelt our peoples melt
   In covert to abide;
Now crouched and still, to cave and hill
   Our jungle barons glide.
Now, stark and plain, Man's oxen strain,
   That draw the new-yoked plough;
Now stripped and dread the dawn is red
   Above the lit *talao.*

Ho! Get to lair! The sun's aflare
   Behind the breathing grass:
And creaking through the young bamboo
   The warning whispers pass.
By day made strange, the woods we range
   With blinking eyes we scan;
While down the skies the wild duck cries:
   "The day—the day to Man!"

The dew is dried that drenched our hide,
   Or washed about our way;
And where we drank, the puddled bank
   Is crisping into clay.
The traitor dark gives up each mark
   Of stretched or hooded claw;
Then hear the call: *"Good rest to all
   That keep the Jungle Law!"*

But no translation can give the effect of it, or the yelping
scorn the four threw into every word of it, as they heard the

trees crash when the men hastily climbed up into the branches, and Buldeo began repeating incantations and charms. Then they lay down and slept, for like all who live by their own exertions, they were of a methodical cast of mind, and no one can work well without sleep.

Meantime, Mowgli was putting the miles behind him, nine to the hour, swinging on, delighted to find himself so fit after all his cramped months among men. The one idea in his head was to get Messua and her husband out of the trap, whatever it was, for he had a natural mistrust of traps. Later on, he promised himself, he would begin to pay his debts to the village at large.

It was at twilight when he saw the well-remembered grazing-grounds, and the *dhâk*-tree where Grey Brother had waited for him on the morning that he killed Shere Khan. Angry as he was at the whole breed and community of Man, something jumped up in his throat and made him catch his breath when he looked at the village roofs. He noticed that every one had come in from the fields unusually early, and that, instead of getting to their evening cooking, they gathered in a crowd under the village tree, and chattered, and shouted.

"Men must always be making traps for men, or they are not content," said Mowgli. "Two nights ago it was Mowgli—but that night seems many rains old. To-night it is Messua and her man. To-morrow, and for very many nights after, it will be Mowgli's turn again."

He crept along outside the wall till he came to Messua's hut, and looked through the window into the room. There lay Messua, gagged, and bound hand and foot, breathing hard, and groaning. Her husband was tied to the gaily painted bedstead. The door of the hut that opened into the street was shut fast, and three or four people were sitting with their backs to it.

Mowgli knew the manners and customs of the villagers very fairly. He argued that so long as they could eat, and talk, and smoke, they would not do anything else, but as soon as they had fed they would begin to be dangerous. Buldeo would be coming in before long, and if his escort had done its duty Buldeo would have a very interesting tale to tell. So he went in through the window, and, stooping over the man and the woman, cut their thongs, pulling out the gags, and looked round the hut for some milk.

Messua was half wild with pain and fear (she had been beaten and stoned all the morning), and Mowgli put his hand over her mouth just in time to stop a scream. Her husband was only bewildered and angry, and sat picking dust and things out of his torn beard.

"I knew—I knew he would come," Messua sobbed at last. "Now do I *know* that he is my son." And she caught Mowgli to her heart. Up to that time Mowgli had been perfectly steady, but here he began to tremble all over, and that surprised him immensely.

"Why are these thongs? Why have they tied thee?" he asked, after a pause.

"To be put to the death for making a son of thee—what else?" said the man, sullenly. "Look! I bleed."

Messua said nothing, but it was at *her* wounds that

Mowgli looked, and they heard him grit his teeth when he saw the blood.

"Whose work is this?" said he. "There is a price to pay."

"The work of all the village. I was too rich. I had too many cattle. *Therefore* she and I are witches, because we gave thee shelter."

"I do not understand. Let Messua tell the tale."

"I gave thee milk, Nathoo. Dost thou remember?" Messua said, timidly. "Because thou wast my son, whom the tiger took, and because I loved thee very dearly. They said that I was thy mother, the mother of a devil, and therefore worthy of death."

"And what is a devil?" said Mowgli. "Death I have seen."

The man looked up gloomily under his eyebrows, but Messua laughed. "See!" she said to her husband. "I knew—I said that he was no sorcerer! He is my son—my son!"

"Son or sorcerer, what good will that do us?" the man answered. "We be as dead already."

"Yonder is the road through the jungle." Mowgli pointed through the window. "Your hands and feet are free. Go now."

"We do not know the jungle, my son, as—as thou knowest," Messua began. "I do not think that I could walk far."

"And the men and women would be upon our backs and drag us here again," said the husband.

"*Hm!*" said Mowgli, and he tickled the palm of his hand with the tip of his skinning-knife. "I have no wish to do harm to any one of this village—*yet*. But I do not think they will stay thee. In a little while they will have much to think upon. Ah!" He lifted his head and listened to shouting and trampling outside. "So they have let Buldeo come home at last?"

"He was sent out this morning to kill thee," Messua cried. "Didst thou meet him?"

"Yes—we—I met him. He has a tale to tell, and while he is talking it there is time to do much. But first I will learn what they mean. Think where ye would go, and tell me when I come back."

He bounded through the window and ran along again outside the wall of the village till he came within earshot of the crowd round the peepul-tree. Buldeo was lying on the ground, coughing and groaning, and every one was asking him questions. His hair had fallen about his shoulders; his hands and legs were skinned from climbing up trees, and he could hardly speak, but he felt the importance of his position keenly. From time to time he said something about devils and singing devils, and magic enchantment, just to give the crowd a taste of what was coming. Then he called for water.

"*Bah!*" said Mowgli. "Chatter—chatter! Talk, talk! Men are blood-brothers of the *Bandar-log*. Now he must wash his mouth with water; now he must blow smoke; and when all that is done he has still his story to tell. They are very wise people—men. They will leave no one to guard Messua till their ears are stuffed with Buldeo's tales. And—I grow as lazy as they!"

He shook himself and glided back to the hut. Just as he

was at the window he felt a touch on his foot.

"Mother," said he, for he knew that tongue well, "what dost *thou* here?"

"I heard my children singing through the woods, and I followed the one I loved best. Little Frog, I have a desire to see that woman who gave thee milk," said Mother Wolf, all wet with the dew.

"They have bound and mean to kill her. I have cut those ties, and she goes with her man through the jungle."

"I also will follow. I am old, but not yet toothless." Mother Wolf reared herself up on end, and looked through the window into the dark of the hut.

In a minute she dropped noiselessly, and all she said was: "I gave thee thy first milk, but Bagheera speaks truth: Man goes to Man at the last."

"Maybe," said Mowgli, with a very unpleasant look on his face, "but to-night I am very far from that trail. Wait here, but do not let her see."

"*Thou* wast never afraid of *me*, little frog," said Mother Wolf, backing into the high grass, and blotting herself out, as she knew how.

"And now," said Mowgli, cheerfully, as he swung into the hut again, "they are all sitting round Buldeo, who is saying that which did not happen. When his talk is finished, they say they will assuredly come here with the Red—with fire and burn you both. And then?"

"I have spoken to my man," said Messua. "Khanhiwara is thirty miles from here, but at Khanhiwara we may find the English—"

"And what pack are they?" said Mowgli.

"I do not know. They be white, and it is said that they govern all the land, and do not suffer people to burn or beat each other without witnesses. If we can get thither to-night we live. Otherwise we die."

"Live then. No man passes the gates to-night. But what does *he* do?" Messua's husband was on his hands and knees digging up the earth in one corner of the hut.

"It is his little money," said Messua. "We can take nothing else."

"Ah, yes. The stuff that passes from hand to hand and never grows warmer. Do they need it outside this place also?" said Mowgli.

The man stared angrily. "He is a fool, and no devil," he muttered. "With the money I can buy a horse. We are too bruised to walk far, and the village will follow us in an hour."

"I say they will *not* follow till I choose, but a horse is well thought of, for Messua is tired." Her husband stood up and knotted the last of the rupees into his waistcloth. Mowgli helped Messua through the window, and the cool night air revived her, but the jungle in the starlight looked very dark and terrible.

"Ye know the trail to Khanhiwara?" Mowgli whispered.

They nodded.

"Good. Remember, now, not to be afraid. And there is no need to go quickly. Only—only there may be some small singing in the jungle behind you and before."

"Think you we would have risked a night in the jungle

through anything less than the fear of burning? It is better to be killed by beasts than by men," said Messua's husband. But Messua looked at Mowgli and smiled.

"I say," Mowgli went on, just as though he were Baloo repeating an old Jungle Law for the hundredth time to an inattentive cub, "I say that not a tooth in the jungle is bared against you, not a foot in the jungle is lifted against you. Neither man nor beast shall stay you till you come within eyeshot of Khanhiwara. There will be a watch about you." He turned quickly to Messua, saying: "*He* does not believe, but thou wilt believe?"

"Aye, surely, my son. Man, ghost, or wolf of the jungle, I believe."

"*He* will be afraid when he hears my people singing. Thou wilt know and understand. Go now, and slowly, for there is no need of any haste. The gates are shut."

Messua flung herself sobbing at Mowgli's feet, but he lifted her very quickly with a shiver. Then she hung about his neck and called him every name of blessing she could think of, but her husband looked enviously across his fields, and said: "*If* we reach Khanhiwara, and I get the ear of the English, I will bring such a lawsuit against the Brahmin and old Buldeo and the others as shall eat this village to the bone. They shall pay me twice over for my crops untilled and my buffaloes unfed. I will have a great justice."

Mowgli laughed. "I do not know what justice is, but— come thou back next rains and see what is left."

They went off towards the jungle, and Mother Wolf leaped from her place of hiding.

"Follow!" said Mowgli. "And look to it that all the jungle knows these two are safe. Give tongue a little. I would call Bagheera."

The long, low howl rose and fell, and Mowgli saw Messua's husband flinch and turn, half minded to run back to the hut.

"Go on," Mowgli shouted, cheerfully. "I said there might be singing. That call will follow up to Khanhiwara. It is the favour of the jungle."

Messua urged her husband forward, and the darkness shut down on them and Mother Wolf as Bagheera rose up almost under Mowgli's feet, trembling with delight of the night that drives the Jungle-People wild.

"I am ashamed of thy brethren," he said, purring.

"What? Did they not sing sweetly to Buldeo?" said Mowgli.

"Too well! Too well! They made even *me* forget my pride, and, by the broken lock that freed me, I went singing through the jungle as though I were out wooing in the spring! Didst thou not hear us?"

"I had other game afoot. Ask Buldeo if he liked the song. But where are the Four? I do not wish one of the man pack to leave the gates to-night."

"What need of the Four, then?" said Bagheera, shifting from foot to foot, his eyes ablaze, and purring louder than ever. "I can hold them, Little Brother. Is it killing at last? The singing and the sight of the men climbing up the trees have made me very ready. Who is Man that we should care for him—the naked brown digger, the hairless and toothless, the eater of earth? I have followed him all day—at noon—in the white sunlight. I herded him as the wolves herd buck. I am Bagheera! Bagheera! Bagheera! As I dance with my shadow so I danced with those men. Look!" The great panther leaped as a kitten leaps at a dead leaf whirling overhead, struck left and right into the empty air, that sung under the strokes, landed noiselessly, and leaped again and again, while the half purr, half growl gathered head as steam rumbles in a boiler. "I am Bagheera—in the jungle—in the night, and my strength is in me. Who shall stay my stroke? Man-cub, with one blow of my paw I could beat thy head flat as a dead frog in the summer!"

"Strike, then!" said Mowgli, in the dialect of the village, *not* the talk of the jungle. And the human words brought Bagheera to a full stop, flung back on his haunches that quivered under him, his head just at the level of Mowgli's. Once more Mowgli stared, as he had stared at the rebellious cubs, full into the beryl-green eyes, till the red glare behind their green went out like the light of a lighthouse shut off twenty miles across the sea, till the eyes dropped, and the big head with them—dropped lower and lower, and the red rasp of a tongue grated on Mowgli's instep.

"Brother—Brother—Brother!" the boy whispered, stroking steadily and lightly from the neck along the heaving back. "Be still, be still! It is the fault of the night, and no fault of thine."

"It was the smells of the night," said Bagheera, penitently. "This air cries aloud to me. But how dost *thou* know?"

Of course the air round an Indian village is full of all kinds of smells, and to any creature who does nearly all his thinking through his nose, smells are as maddening as music and drugs are to human beings. Mowgli gentled the panther for a few minutes longer, and he lay down like a cat before a fire, his paws tucked under his breast, and his eyes half shut.

"Thou art of the jungle and *not* of the jungle," he said at last. "And I am only a black panther. But I love thee, Little Brother."

"They are very long at their talk under the tree," Mowgli said, without noticing the last sentence. "Buldeo must have told many tales. They should come soon to drag the woman and her man out of the trap and put them into the Red Flower. They will find that trap sprung. Ho! Ho!"

"Nay, listen," said Bagheera. "The fever is out of my blood now. Let them find *me* there! Few would leave their houses after meeting me. It is not the first time I have been in a cage, and I do not think they will tie *me* with cords."

"Be wise, then," said Mowgli, laughing, for he was beginning to feel as reckless as the panther, who had glided into the hut.

"*Pah!*" Bagheera puffed. "This place is rank with Man, but here is just such a bed as they gave me to lie upon in the king's cages at Oodeypore. Now I lie down." Mowgli heard the strings of the cot crack under the great brute's weight. "By the broken lock that freed me, they will think they have caught big game! Come and sit beside me, Little Brother. We will give them 'good hunting' together!"

"No, I have another thought in my stomach. The man pack shall not know what share I have in the sport. Make thine own hunt. I do not wish to see them."

"Be it so," said Bagheera. "Now they come!"

The conference under the peepul-tree had been growing noisier and noisier, at the far end of the village. It broke in wild yells, and a rush up the street of men and women, waving clubs and bamboos and sickles and knives. Buldeo and the Brahmin were at the head of it, but the mob was close at their heels, and they cried: "The witch and the wizard! Let us see if hot coins will make them confess! Burn the hut over their heads! We will teach them to shelter wolf-devils! Nay, beat them first! Torches! More torches! Buldeo, heat the gun-barrel!"

Here was some little difficulty with the catch of the door. It had been very firmly fastened, but the crowd tore it away bodily, and the light of the torches streamed into the room where, stretched at full length on the bed, his paws crossed and lightly hung down over one end, black as the pit and terrible as a demon, was Bagheera. There was one half-minute of desperate silence, as the front ranks of the crowd clawed and tore their way back from the threshold, and in that minute Bagheera raised his head and yawned— elaborately, carefully, and ostentatiously—as he would yawn when he wished to insult an equal. The fringed lips drew back and up; the red tongue curled; the lower jaw dropped and dropped till you could see half-way down the hot gullet; and the gigantic dogteeth stood clear to the pit of the gums till they rang together, upper and under, with the snick of steel-faced wards shooting home round the edges of a safe. Next minute the street was empty. Bagheera had leaped back through the window, and stood at Mowgli's side, while a yelling, screaming torrent scrambled and tumbled one over another in their panic haste to get to their huts.

"They will not stir till the day comes," said Bagheera, quietly. "And now?"

The silence of the afternoon sleep seemed to have overtaken the village, but, as they listened, they could hear the sound of heavy grain-boxes being dragged over earthen floors and pushed against doors. Bagheera was quite right. The village would not stir till daylight. Mowgli sat still and thought, and his face grew darker and darker.

"What have I done?" said Bagheera, at last, fawning.

"Nothing but great good. Watch them now till the day. I sleep." Mowgli ran off into the jungle, and dropped across a rock, and slept and slept the day round, and the night back again.

When he waked, Bagheera was at his side, and there lay a newly killed buck at his feet. Bagheera watched curiously while Mowgli went to work with his skinning-knife, ate and drank, and turned over with his chin in his hands.

"The man and the woman came safe within eye-shot of Khanhiwara," Bagheera said. "Thy mother sent the word back by Chil. They found a horse before midnight of the night they were freed, and went very quickly. Is not that well?"

"That is well," said Mowgli.

"And thy man pack in the village did not stir till the sun was high this morning. Then they ate their food and ran back quickly to their houses."

"Did they, by chance, see thee?"

"It may have been. I was rolling in the dust before the gate at dawn, and I may have made also some small song to myself. Now, Little Brother, there is nothing more to do. Come hunting with me and Baloo. He has new hives that he wishes to show, and we all desire thee back again as of old. Take off that look which makes even *me* afraid. The man and woman will not be put into the Red Flower, and all goes well in the jungle. Is it not true? Let us forget the man pack."

"They shall be forgotten—in a little while. Where does Hathi feed to-night?"

"Where he chooses. Who can answer for the Silent One? But why? What is there Hathi can do which we cannot?"

"Bid him and his three sons come here to me."

"But, indeed, and truly, Little Brother, it is not—it is not seemly to say 'Come' and 'Go' to Hathi. Remember, he is the master of the jungle, and before the man pack changed the look on thy face, he taught thee a Master Word of the Jungle."

"That is all one. I have a Master Word for him now. Bid him come to Mowgli the Frog, and if he does not hear at first, bid him come because of the sack of the fields of Bhurtpore."

"The sack of the fields of Bhurtpore," Bagheera repeated two or three times to make sure. "I go. Hathi can but be angry at the worst, and I would give a moon's hunting to hear a Master Word that compels the Silent One."

He went away, leaving Mowgli stabbing furiously with his skinning-knife into the earth. Mowgli had never seen human blood in his life before till he had seen, and—what meant much more to him—smelled Messua's blood on the thongs that bound her. And Messua had been kind to him, and, so far as he knew anything about love, he loved Messua as completely as he hated the rest of mankind. But deeply as he loathed them, their talk, their cruelty, and their cowardice, not for anything the jungle had to offer could he bring himself to take a human life, and have that terrible scent of blood back again in his nostrils. His plan was simpler but much more thorough, and he laughed to himself when he thought that it was one of old Buldeo's tales told under the peepul-tree in the evening that had put the idea into his head.

"It *was* a Master Word," Bagheera whispered in his ear. "They were feeding by the river, and they obeyed as though they were bullocks. Look, where they come now!"

Hathi and his three sons had appeared in their usual way, without a sound. The mud of the river was still fresh on their flanks, and Hathi was thoughtfully chewing the green stem of a young plantain-tree that he had gouged up with his tusks. But every line in his vast body showed to Bagheera, who could see things when he came across them, that it was not the master of the jungle speaking to a man-cub, but one who was afraid coming before one who was not. His three sons rolled side by side, behind their father.

Mowgli hardly lifted his head as Hathi gave him "Good hunting." He kept him swinging and rocking, and shifting from one foot to another, for a long time before he spoke, and when he opened his mouth it was to Bagheera, not to the elephants.

"I will tell a tale that was told to me by the hunter ye hunted to-day," said Mowgli. "It concerns an elephant, old and wise, who fell into a trap, and the sharpened stake in the pit scarred him from a little above his heel to the crest of his shoulder, leaving a white mark." Mowgli threw out his hand, and as Hathi wheeled the moonlight showed a long white scar on his slaty side, as though he had been struck with a red-hot whip. "Men came to take him from the trap," Mowgli continued, "but he broke his ropes, for he was strong, and he went away till his wound was healed. Then came he, angry, by night to the fields of those hunters. And I remember now that he had three sons. These things happened many, many rains ago, and very far away—among the fields of Bhurtpore. What came to those fields at the next reaping, Hathi?"

"They were reaped by me and by my three sons," said Hathi.

"And to the ploughing that follows the reaping?" said Mowgli.

"There was no ploughing," said Hathi.

"And to the men that live by the green crops on the ground?" said Mowgli.

"They went away."

"And to the huts in which the men slept?" said Mowgli.

"We tore the roofs to pieces, and the jungle swallowed

up the walls," said Hathi.

"And what more, besides?" said Mowgli.

"As much good ground as I can walk over in two nights from the east to the west, and from the north to the south as much as I can walk over in three nights, the jungle took. We let in the jungle upon five villages, and in those villages, and in their lands, the grazing-ground and the soft crop-grounds, there is not one man to-day who gets his food from the ground. That was the sack of the fields of Bhurtpore, which I and my three sons did. And now I ask, man-cub, how the news of it came to thee?" said Hathi.

"A man told me. And now I see even Buldeo can speak truth. It was well done, Hathi with the white mark, but the second time it shall be done better, for the reason that there is a man to direct. Thou knowest the village of the man pack that cast me out? They are idle, senseless, and cruel; they play with their mouths, and they do not kill their weaker for food, but for sport. When they are full-fed they would throw their own breed into the Red Flower. This I have seen. It is not well that they should live here any more. I hate them!"

"Kill, then," said the youngest of Hathi's three sons, picking up a tuft of grass, dusting it against his fore legs, and throwing it away, while his little red eyes glanced furtively from side to side.

"What good are white bones to me?" Mowgli answered furiously. "Am I the cub of a wolf to play in the sun with a raw head? I have killed Shere Khan, and his hide rots on the Council Rock, but—but I do not know whither Shere

Khan is gone, and my stomach is still empty. Now I will take that which I can see and touch. Let in the jungle upon that village, Hathi!"

Bagheera shivered, and cowered down. He could understand, if the worst came to the worst, a quick rush down the village street, and a right and left blow into a crowd, or a crafty killing of men as they ploughed in the twilight, but this scheme deliberately blotting out an entire village from the eyes of man and beast frightened him. Now he saw why Mowgli had sent for Hathi. No one but the long-lived elephant could plan and carry through such a war.

"Let them run as the men ran from the fields of Bhurtpore, till we have the rain-water for the only plough, and the noise of the rain on the thick leaves for the pattering of their spindles—till Bagheera and I lair in the house of the Brahmin, and the buck drink at the tank behind the temple! Let in the jungle, Hathi!"

"But I—but we have no quarrel with them, and it needs the red rage of great pain ere we tear down the places where men sleep," said Hathi, rocking doubtfully.

"Are ye the only Eaters of Grass in the jungle? Drive in your peoples. Let the deer and the pig and the nilghai look to it. Ye need never show a hand's-breadth of hide till the fields are naked. Let in the jungle, Hathi!"

"There will be no killing? My tusks were red at the sack of the fields of Bhurtpore, and I would not wake that smell again."

"Nor I. I do not wish even their bones to lie on our clean earth. Let them go find a fresh lair. They cannot stay here!

I have seen and smelled the blood of the woman that gave me food—the woman whom they would have killed but for me. Only the smell of the new grass on their door-steps can take away that smell. It burns in my mouth. Let in the jungle, Hathi!"

"Ah!" said Hathi. "So did the scar of the stake burn on my hide till we watched the villages die under in the spring growth. Now I see. Thy war shall be our war. We will let in the jungle."

Mowgli had hardly time to catch his breath—he was shaking all over with rage and hate—before the place where the elephants had stood was empty, and Bagheera was looking at him with terror.

"By the broken lock that freed me!" said the black panther at last. "Art *thou* the naked thing I spoke for in the pack when all was young? Master of the jungle, when my strength goes, speak for me—speak for Baloo—speak for us all! We are cubs before thee! Snapped twigs under foot! Fawns that have lost their doe!"

The idea of Bagheera being a stray fawn upset Mowgli altogether, and he laughed and caught his breath, and sobbed and laughed again, till he had to jump into a pool to make himself stop. Then he swam round and round, ducking in and out of the bars of the moonlight like the frog, his namesake.

By this time Hathi and his three sons had turned, each to one point of the compass, and were striding silently down the valleys a mile away. They went on and on for two days' march—that is to say, a long sixty miles—through the jungle, while every step they took, and every wave of their trunks, was known and noted and talked over by Mang and Chil and the Monkey-People and all the birds. Then they began to feed, and fed quietly for a week or so. Hathi and his sons are like Kaa the Rock Python. They never hurry till they have to.

At the end of that time—and none knew who had started it—a rumour went through the jungle that there was better food and water to be found in such and such a valley. The pigs—who, of course, will go to the ends of the earth for a full meal—moved first by companies, scuffling over the rocks, and the deer followed, with the little wild foxes that live on the dead and dying of the herds; and the heavy-shouldered nilghai moved parallel with the deer, and the wild buffaloes of the swamps came after the nilghai. The least little thing would have turned the scattered, straggling droves that grazed and sauntered and drank and grazed again, but whenever there was an alarm some one would rise up and soothe them. At one time it would be Sahi the Porcupine, full of news of good feed just a little farther on; at another Mang would cry cheerily and flap down a glade to show it was all empty; or Baloo, his mouth full of roots, would shamble alongside a wavering line and half frighten, half romp it clumsily back to the proper road. Very many creatures broke back or ran away or lost interest, but very many were left to go forward. At the end of another ten days or so the situation was this. The deer and the pig and the nilghai were milling round and round in a circle of eight or ten miles' radius, while the Eaters of Flesh skirmished round its edge. And the centre of that circle was the village, and round the village the crops were ripening, and in the crops sat men on what they call *machans*—platforms like pigeon-perches, made of sticks at the top of four poles—to scare away birds and other stealers. Then the deer were coaxed no more. The Eaters of Flesh were close behind them, and forced them forward and inward.

It was a dark night when Hathi and his three sons slipped down from the jungle, and broke off the poles of the *machans* with their trunks, and they fell as a snapped stalk of hemlock in bloom falls, and the men that tumbled from them heard the deep gurgling of the elephants in their ears. Then the vanguard of the bewildered armies of the deer broke down and flooded into the village grazing-grounds and the ploughed fields; and the sharp-hoofed, rooting wild pig came with them, and what the deer left the pig spoiled, and from time to time an alarm of wolves would shake the herds, and they would rush to and fro desperately, treading down the young barley, and cutting flat the banks of the irrigating channels. Before the dawn broke the pressure on the outside of the circle gave way at one point. The Eaters of Flesh had fallen back and left an open path to the south, and drove upon drove of buck fled along it. Others, who were bolder, lay up in the thickets to finish their meal next night.

But the work was practically done. When the villagers looked in the morning they saw their crops were lost. That meant death if they did not get away, for they lived year in and year out as near to starvation as the jungle was near to them. When the buffaloes were sent to graze the hungry brutes found that the deer had cleared the grazing-grounds, and so wandered into the jungle and drifted off with their wild mates; and when twilight fell the three or four ponies that belonged to the village lay in their stables with their heads beaten in. Only Bagheera could have given those strokes, and only Bagheera could have thought of insolently dragging the last carcass to the open street.

The villagers had no heart to make fires in the fields that night, so Hathi and his three sons went gleaning among what was left, and where Hathi gleans there is no need to follow. The men decided to live on their stored seed-corn until the rains had fallen, and then to take work as servants till they could catch up with the lost year. But as the grain-dealer was thinking of his well-filled crates of corn, and the prices he would levy at the sale of it, Hathi's sharp tusks were picking out the corner of his mud-house, and smashing up the big wicker-chest, leeped with cow-dung, where the precious stuff lay.

When that last loss was discovered, it was the Brahmin's turn to speak. He had prayed to his own gods without answer. It might be, he said, that, unconsciously, the village had offended some one of the gods of the jungle, for, beyond doubt, the jungle was against them. So they sent for the head-man of the nearest tribes of wandering Gonds—little, wise, and very black hunters, living in the deep jungle, whose fathers came of the oldest race in India—the aboriginal owners of the land. They made the Gond welcome with what they had, and he stood on one leg, his bow

in his hand, and two or three poisoned arrows stuck
through his top-knot, looking half afraid and half contemptuously at the anxious villagers and their ruined fields.
They wished to know whether his gods—the Old Gods—
were angry with them, and what sacrifices should be offered. The Gond said nothing, but picked up a trail of the
karela, the vine that bears the bitter wild gourd, and laced
it to and fro across the temple door in the face of the staring
red Hindu image. Then he pushed with his hand in the
open air along the road to Khanhiwara, and went back to
his jungle, and watched the Jungle-People drifting
through it. He knew that when the jungle moves only
white men can hope to turn it aside.

There was no need to ask his meaning. The wild gourd
would grow where they had worshipped their god, and the
sooner they saved themselves the better.

But it is hard to tear a village from its moorings. They
stayed on as long as any summer food was left to them, and
they tried to gather nuts in the jungle, but shadows with
glaring eyes watched them, and rolled before them even at
mid-day, and when they ran back afraid to their walls, on
the tree-trunks they had passed not five minutes before the
bark would be striped and chiselled with the stroke of some
great taloned paw. The more they kept to their village, the
bolder grew the wild things that gambolled and bellowed
on the grazing-grounds by the Wainganga. They had no
heart to patch and plaster the rear walls of the empty byres
that backed on to the jungle; the wild pig trampled them
down, and the knotty-rooted vines hurried after and threw

their elbows over the new-won ground, and the coarse grass bristled behind the vines. The unmarried men ran away first, and carried the news far and near that the village was doomed. Who could fight, they said, against the jungle, or the gods of the jungle, when the very village cobra had left his hole in the platform under the peepul? So their little commerce with the outside world shrank as the trodden paths across the open grew fewer and fainter. And the nightly trumpetings of Hathi and his three sons ceased to trouble them; they had no more to go. The crop on the ground and the seed in the ground had been taken. The outlying fields were already losing their shape, and it was time to throw themselves on the charity of the English at Khanhiwara.

Native fashion, they delayed their departure from one day to another till the first rains caught them and the un-mended roofs let in a flood, and the grazing-ground stood ankle deep, and all green things came on with a rush after the heat of the summer. Then they waded out—men, women, and children—through the blinding hot rain of the morning, but turned naturally for one farewell look at their homes.

They heard, as the last burdened family filed through the gate, a crash of falling beams and thatch behind the walls. They saw a shiny, snaky black trunk lifted for an instant, scattering sodden thatch. It disappeared, and there was another crash, followed by a squeal. Hathi had been plucking off the roofs of the huts as you pluck water-lilies, and a rebounding beam had pricked him. He needed only this to unchain his full strength, for of all things in the jungle the wild elephant enraged is the most wantonly destructive. He kicked backwards at a mud wall that crumbled at the stroke, and, crumbling, melted to yellow mud under the torrents of rain. Then he wheeled and squealed, and tore through the narrow streets, leaning against the huts right and left, shivering the crazy doors, and crumpling up the eaves, while his three sons raged behind as they had raged at the sack of the fields of Bhurtpore.

"The jungle will swallow these shells," said a quiet voice in the wreckage. "It is the outer walls that must lie down." And Mowgli, with the rain sluicing over his bare shoulders and arms, leaped back from a wall that was settling like a tired buffalo.

"All in good time," panted Hathi. "Oh, but my tusks were red at Bhurtpore! To the outer wall, children! With the head! Together! Now!"

The four pushed side by side. The outer wall bulged, split, and fell, and the villagers, dumb with horror, saw the savage, clay-streaked heads of the wreckers in the ragged gap. Then they fled, houseless and foodless, down the valley, as their village, shredded and tossed and trampled, melted behind them.

A month later the place was a dimpled mound, covered with soft, green young stuff, and by the end of the rains there was the roaring jungle in full blast on the spot that had been under plough not six months before.

MOWGLI'S SONG AGAINST PEOPLE

I will let loose against you the fleet-footed vines—
I will call in the jungle to stamp out your lines!
   The roofs shall fade before it,
     The house-beams shall fall,
   And the *karela,* the bitter *karela,*
     Shall cover it all!

In the gates of these your councils my people shall sing,
In the doors of these your garners the Bat-Folk shall cling;
   And the snake shall be your watchman,
     By a hearthstone unswept;
   For the *karela,* the bitter *karela,*
     Shall fruit where ye slept!

Ye shall not see my strikers; ye shall hear them and guess;
By night, before the moon-rise, I will send for my cess,
   And the wolf shall be your herdsman
     By a landmark removed,
   For the *karela,* the bitter *karela,*
     Shall seed where ye loved!

I will reap your fields before you at the hands of a host;
Ye shall glean behind my reapers for the bread that is lost;
   And the deer shall be your oxen
     By a headland untilled,
   For the *karela,* the bitter *karela,*
     Shall leaf where ye build!

I have untied against you the club-footed vines,
I have sent in the jungle to swamp out your lines.
   The trees—the trees are on you!
     The house-beams shall fall,
  And the *karela*, the bitter *karela*,
    Shall cover you all!

Interpretive Questions

1. Why in the course of destroying the village does Mowgli become master of the jungle?

2. When caught up in the smells of the night, why does Bagheera brag of his ability to kill Mowgli? (85)

3. If the Free Hunters feel such scorn and contempt for Man, why do they still respect human beings and think them "wisest of all"? (69)

PLOT PLOT PLOT PLOT PLOT PLO
OT PLOT PLOT PLOT PLOT PL
LOT PLOT PLOT PL OT PLOT F
OT PLOT PL OT PLOT F
PLOT PLO PLOT PLO
OT PL PL PL
PLO **Thinking** LOT
DI DI
Interpretively
OT PLOT PLOT PLOT PLOT F
PLOT PLOT PLOT PLOT PLO
OT PLOT PLOT PLOT PL
PLOT PLOT PLOT PLOT P
PLOT PLOT PLOT PLOT
OT PLOT PLOT PLOT PLO
OT PLOT PLOT P **Thin**
PLOT PLOT
OT PLOT PLOT **Interpr**
PLOT PLOT PLOT PLOT PLOT
PLOT PLOT PLOT PLOT PLO
OT PLOT PLOT PLOT PL
OT PLOT PLOT PLOT F
PLOT PLOT PLOT PLO
OT PLOT PLOT PLOT PL
PLOT PLOT PLOT PLOT
PLOT PLOT PLOT PLO
PLOT PLOT PL
Thinking OT PLOT F
iterpretively PLO
PLOT PLOT PLOT PLOT
PLOT PLOT PLOT PLOT PLO
PLOT PLOT PLOT PLO
OT PLOT PLOT PLOT P
OT PLOT PLOT PLOT
OT PLOT PLO
PLOT PLOT F **Thinki**
OT PLOT PLOT
PLOT PLOT **Interpret**
PLOT PLO
OT PLOT PLOT PLOT PLOT PL
T PLOT PLOT PLOT F
T PLOT PLOT PLOT F
OT PLOT PLOT PLO
iinking PLOT PLOT PL
OT PLOT PLO
rpretively PLOT PLO
PLOT PL
OT PLOT PLOT PLOT PLOT F
OT PLOT PLOT PLOT PLOT F
PLOT PLOT PLOT PLO
OT PLOT PLOT PLO PL
PLOT PLOT PLOT P OT
PLOT PLOT PLOT PLO
OT PLOT PL
OT PLOT P **Thinkin**
OT PLO
PLOT F **Interpretiv**
OT PLOT PLOT PLOT PLOT PL
PLOT PLOT PLOT PLOT PL
PLOT PLOT PLOT PLOT PLO
OT PLOT PLOT PLOT PLOT F
OT PL OT PLOT PLOT F
OT PL OT PLOT PLOT F
PLOT PLOT PLOT
Thinking PLOT PL
OT PLOT
iterpretively PLO
T PL

Thinking Interpretively: Plot

Many stories are about people with problems or in conflict. Toward the beginning of a story, you will usually find a character who is in a difficult or complicated situation. By the story's end, through the character's own actions—and as a result of what the other characters do—his or her situation has changed. The middle part of the story tells us about those things that had to happen to bring about the change. *Plot* is the arrangement of all the happenings in a story from the beginning through the middle to the end.

In thinking about a story's plot, we want not only to follow *what* happens, but also to be able to say *why* things happen as they do. In "Letting in the Jungle," the major action of the story revolves around Mowgli's conflict with the villagers—their efforts to kill him, Messua, and Messua's husband. The story ends when Mowgli arranges not only for Messua's escape, but also for the destruction of the village by Hathi and his sons and the other jungle animals. *But why must Mowgli arrange for such an extreme solution?* One way to understand the underlying "why's" of a plot is to examine a character's reasons for acting. Let us try to "untie the knot" of Mowgli's conflict with the villagers by looking more closely at his relationships with others, especially his friendship with Bagheera.

The story begins with Mowgli returning to his wolf family after being cast out by the man pack. But Mowgli does not feel at home with the wolves either. When Akela calls him a man, Mowgli reacts very angrily, throwing his knife at the Lone Wolf. There is tension, too, in Mowgli's relationship with Bagheera. When Mowgli prevents his four brother wolves from killing Buldeo—asking furiously, "Am I to give reason for all I choose to do?"—Bagheera mutters under his whiskers,

"That is Man! There speaks Man!" (p. 69) *Where does Mowgli properly belong—with the Jungle-People or with the man pack?* Mowgli's struggle with this problem— and with his changing relationships with the jungle animals—forms a central part of how he reacts to the villagers.

Once we have identified an important conflict or "knot" in a story, we can follow it through to its resolution or *denouement*, which is a French word that literally means "untying." For example, in exploring further Mowgli's anger at the villagers, we noticed that as his rage intensifies, so does his power in the jungle. When Mowgli succeeds in getting Hathi to agree to destroy the village, Bagheera views Mowgli with awe and terror. When the story ends, Mowgli has established himself as the new master of the jungle. Is the knot untied? It would seem that Mowgli has resolved his feelings toward the villagers, that he has found his rightful place. *But why,* we wondered, *does Mowgli think that the complete destruction of the village is a suitable revenge for the harm done to him and Messua? And why is Mowgli furious at the suggestion of Hathi's youngest son that he kill his human enemies?* Asking such questions —looking closely at the "why's" of a story's plot—can often be the first step toward raising important interpretive issues. ▮

The Jungle Books

The Spring Running

The second year after the great fight with Red Dog and the death of Akela,* Mowgli must have been nearly seventeen years old. He looked older, for hard exercise, the best of good eating, and baths whenever he felt in the least hot or dusty had given him strength and growth far beyond his age. He could swing by one hand from a top branch for half an hour at a time, when he had occasion to look along the tree-roads. He could stop a young buck in mid-gallop and throw him sideways by the head. He could even jerk over the big blue wild boars that lived in the Marshes of the North. The Jungle-People, who used to fear him for his wits, feared him now for his mere strength, and when he moved quietly on his own affairs the whisper of his coming cleared the wood-path. And yet the look in his eyes was always gentle. Even when he fought his eyes never glazed as Bagheera's did. They only grew more and more interested and excited, and that was one of the things that Bagheera himself did not understand.

He asked Mowgli about it, and the boy laughed and said:

---

*The story "Red Dog" tells how Mowgli leads the victorious fight against a huge pack of rampaging dholes who threaten the Seeonee wolves. In the battle, Akela is killed.

"When I miss the kill I am angry. When I go empty for two days I am very angry. Do not my eyes talk then?"

"The mouth is hungry," said Bagheera, "but the eyes say nothing. Hunting, eating, or swimming, it is all one—like a stone in wet or dry weather." Mowgli looked at him lazily from under his long eyelashes, and, as usual, the panther's head dropped. Bagheera knew his master.

They were lying out far up the side of a hill overlooking the Wainganga, and the morning mists lay below them in bands of white and green. As the sun rose they changed into bubbling seas of red and gold, churned off and let the low rays stripe the dried grass on which Mowgli and Bagheera were resting. It was the end of the cold weather, the leaves and the trees looked worn and faded, and there was a dry ticking rustle when the wind blew. A little leaf tap-tap-tapped furiously against a twig as a single leaf caught in a current will. It roused Bagheera, for he snuffed the morning air with a deep hollow cough, threw himself on his back, and struck with his fore paws at the nodding leaf above.

"The year turns," he said. "The jungle goes forward. The Time of New Talk is near. That leaf knows. It is very good."

"The grass is dry," Mowgli answered, pulling up a tuft. "Even Eye-of-the-Spring [that is a little, trumpet-shaped waxy red flower that runs in and out among the grasses] —even Eye-of-the-Spring is shut and . . . Bagheera, is it well for the Black Panther so to lie on his back and beat with his paws in the air as though he were the tree-cat?"

"Aowh!" said Bagheera. He seemed to be thinking of other things.

"I say, *is* it well for the Black Panther so to mouth and cough and howl and roll? Remember, we be the masters of the jungle, thou and I."

"Indeed, yes. I hear, man-cub." Bagheera rolled over hurriedly, and sat up, the dust on his ragged black flanks. (He was just casting his winter coat.) "We be surely the masters of the jungle! Who is so strong as Mowgli? Who so wise?" There was a curious drawl in the voice that made Mowgli turn to see whether by any chance the black panther were making fun of him, for the jungle is full of words that sound like one thing but mean another. "I said we be beyond question the masters of the jungle," Bagheera repeated. "Have I done wrong? I did not know that the man-cub no longer lay upon the ground. Does he fly, then?"

Mowgli sat with his elbows on his knees looking out across the valley at the daylight. Somewhere down in the woods below a bird was trying over in a husky, reedy voice the first few notes of his spring song. It was no more than a shadow of the full-throated tumbling call he would be crying later, but Bagheera heard it.

"I said the Time of New Talk was near," growled the panther, switching his tail.

"I hear," Mowgli answered. "Bagheera, why dost thou shake all over? The sun is warm."

"That is Ferao, the scarlet woodpecker," said Bagheera. "*He* has not forgotten. Now I too must remember my song." And he began purring and crooning to himself, harking back dissatisfied again and again.

"There is no game afoot," said Mowgli, lazily.

"Little Brother, are *both* thine ears stopped? That is no killing-word but my song that I make ready against the need."

"I had forgotten. I shall know when the Time of New Talk is here, because then thou and the others run away and leave me single-foot." Mowgli spoke rather savagely.

"But, indeed, Little Brother," Bagheera began, "we do not always—"

"I say ye do," said Mowgli, shooting out his forefinger angrily. "Ye *do* run away, and I, who am the master of the jungle, must needs walk single-foot. How was it last season, when I would gather sugar-cane from the fields of a man pack? I sent a runner—I sent thee!—to Hathi bidding him to come upon such a night and pluck the sweet grass for me with his trunk."

"He came only two nights later," said Bagheera, cowering a little, "and of that long sweet grass that pleased thee so, he gathered more than any man-cub could eat in all the nights of the rains. His was no fault of mine."

"He did not come upon the night when I sent him the word. No, he was trumpeting and running and roaring through valleys in the moonlight. His trail was like the trail of three elephants, for he would not hide among the trees. He danced in the moonlight before the houses of the man pack. I saw him, and yet he would not come to me; and *I* am the master of the jungle!"

"It was the Time of New Talk," said the panther, always

very humble. "Perhaps, Little Brother, thou didst not that time call him by a Master Word? Listen to Ferao!"

Mowgli's bad temper seemed to have boiled itself away. He lay back with his head on his arms, his eyes shut. "I do not know—nor do I care," he said sleepily. "Let us sleep, Bagheera. My stomach is heavy in me. Make me a rest for my head."

The panther lay down again with a sigh, because he could hear Ferao practising and repractising his song against the Spring-time of New Talk, as they say.

In an Indian jungle the seasons slide one into the other almost without division. There seem to be only two—the wet and the dry—but if you look closely below the torrents of rain and the clouds of char and dust you will find all four going round in their regular order. Spring is the most wonderful, because she has not to cover a clean bare field with new leaves and flowers, but to drive before her and to put away the hanging-on, over-surviving raffle of half-green things which the gentle winter has suffered to live, and to make the partly dressed, stale earth feel new and young once more. And this she does so well that there is no spring in the world like the jungle spring.

There is one day when all things are tired, and the very smells as they drift on the heavy air are old and used. One cannot explain, but it feels so. Then there is another day—to the eye nothing whatever has changed—when all the smells are new and delightful and the whiskers of the Jungle-People quiver to their roots, and the winter hair comes away from their sides in long draggled locks. Then, perhaps, a little rain falls, and all the trees and the bushes and the bamboos and the mosses and the juicy-leaved plants wake with a noise of growing that you can almost hear, and under this noise runs, day and night, a deep hum. *That* is the noise of the spring—a vibrating boom which is neither bees nor falling water nor the wind in the tree-tops, but the purring of the warm, happy world.

Up to this year Mowgli had always delighted in the turn of the seasons. It was he who generally saw the first Eye-of-the-Spring deep down among the grasses, and the first bank of spring clouds which are like nothing else in the jungle. His voice could be heard in all sorts of wet star-lighted blossoming places, helping the big frogs through their choruses, or mocking the little upside-down owls that hoot through the white nights. Like all his people, spring was the season he chose for his flittings—moving for mere joy of rushing through the warm air, thirty, forty, or fifty miles between twilight and the morning star, and coming back panting and laughing and wreathed with strange flowers. The Four did not follow him on these wild ringings of the jungle, but went off to sing songs with other wolves. The Jungle-People are very busy in the spring, and Mowgli could hear them grunting and screaming and whistling according to their kind. Their voices then are different from their voices at other times of the year, and that is one of the reasons why spring is called the Time of New Talk.

But that spring, as he told Bagheera, his stomach was new in him. Ever since the bamboo shoots turned spotty-brown he had been looking forward to the morning when the smells should change. But when that morning came, and Mor the Peacock, blazing in bronze and blue and gold, cried it aloud all along the misty woods, and Mowgli opened his mouth to send on the cry, the words choked between his teeth, and a feeling came over him that began at his toes and ended in his hair—a feeling of pure unhappiness—and he looked himself over to be sure that he had not trodden on a thorn. Mor cried the new smells, the other birds took it over, and from the rocks by the Wainganga he heard Bagheera's hoarse scream—something between the scream of an eagle and the neighing of a horse. There was a yelling and scattering of *Bandar-log* in the new-budding branches above, and there stood Mowgli, his chest filled to answer Mor, sinking in little gasps as the breath was driven out of it by this unhappiness.

He stared, but he could see no more than the mocking *Bandar-log* scudding through the trees, and Mor, his tail spread in full splendour, dancing on the slopes below.

"The smells have changed," screamed Mor. "Good hunting, Little Brother! Where is thy answer?"

"Little Brother, good hunting!" whistled Chil the Kite and his mate swooping down together. The two baffed under Mowgli's nose so close that a pinch of downy white feathers brushed out.

A light spring rain—elephant-rain they call it—drove across the jungle in a belt half a mile wide, left the new leaves wet and nodding behind, and died out in a double rainbow and a light roll of thunder. The spring-hum broke out for a minute and was silent, but all the Jungle-Folk seemed to be giving tongue at once. All except Mowgli.

"I have eaten good food," he said to himself. "I have drunk good water. Nor does my throat burn and grow small, as it did when I bit the blue-spotted root that Oo the Turtle said was clean food. But my stomach is heavy, and I have, for no cause, given very bad talk to Bagheera and others, people of the jungle and my people. Now, too, I am hot and now I am cold, and now I am neither hot nor cold, but angry with that which I cannot see. *Huhu!* It is time to make a running! To-night I will cross the ranges; yes, I will make a spring running to the Marshes of the North and back again. I have hunted too easily too long. The Four shall come with me, for they grow as fat as white grubs."

He called, but never one of the Four answered. They were far beyond earshot, singing over the spring songs— the moon and sambur songs—with the wolves of the pack, for in the spring-time the Jungle-People make little difference between the day and the night. He gave the sharp barking note, but his only answer was the mocking *maiou* of the little spotted tree-cat winding in and out among the branches for early birds' nests. At this he shook all over with rage and half drew his knife. Then he became very haughty, though there was no one to see him, and stalked severely down the hillside, chin up and eyebrows down. But never a single one of his people asked him a question, for they were all too busy with their own affairs.

"Yes," said Mowgli to himself, though in his heart he knew that he had no reason. "Let the red dhole come from the Dekkan or the Red Flower dance among the bamboos, and all the jungle runs whining to Mowgli calling him great elephant names. But now, because Eye-of-the-Spring is red, and Mor, forsooth, must show his naked legs in some spring-dance, the jungle goes mad as Tabaqui. . . . By the bull that bought me, am I the master of the jungle or am I not? Be silent! What do ye here?"

A couple of young wolves of the pack were cantering down a path looking for open ground in which to fight. (You will remember that the Law of the Jungle forbids fighting where the pack can see.) Their neck-bristles were as stiff as wire, and they bayed, furiously crouching for the first grapple. Mowgli leaped forward, caught one out-stretched throat in either hand, expecting to fling the creatures backwards, as he had often done in games or pack hunts. But he had never before interfered with a spring fight. The two leaped forward and dashed him aside to the earth, and without a word to waste rolled over and over close locked.

Mowgli was on his feet almost before he fell, his knife and his white teeth were bared, and at that minute he would have killed both for no reason but that they were fighting when he wished them to be quiet, although every wolf has full right under the Law to fight. He danced round them with lowered shoulders and quivering hand ready to send in a double blow when the first flurry of the scuffle should be over, but while he waited the strength seemed to go out of his body, the knife point lowered, and he sheathed the knife and watched.

"I have eaten poison," he said at last. "Since I broke up the council with the Red Flower—since I killed Shere Khan none of the pack would fling me aside. And these be only tail-wolves in the pack, little hunters. My strength is gone from me, and presently I shall die. O, Mowgli, why dost thou not kill them both?"

The fight went on till one wolf ran away, and Mowgli was left alone on the torn and bloody ground, looking now at his knife, and now at his legs and arms, while the feeling of unhappiness he had never known before covered him as water covers a log.

He killed early that evening and ate but little, so as to be in good fettle for his spring running, and he ate alone because all the Jungle-People were away singing or fighting. It was a perfect white night, as they call it. All green things seemed to have made a month's growth since the morning. The branch that was yellow-leaved the day before dripped sap when Mowgli broke it. The mosses curled deep and warm over his feet, the young grass had no cutting edges, and all the voices of the jungle boomed like one deep harp-string touched by the moon—the full Moon of New Talk, who splashed her light full on rock and pool, slipped it between trunk and creeper, and sifted it through the million leaves. Unhappy as he was, Mowgli sang aloud with pure delight as he settled into his stride. It was more like flying than anything else, for he had chosen the long downward slope that leads to the northern marshes through the heart of the main jungle, where the springy ground deadened the fall of his feet. A man-taught man would have picked his way with many stumbles through the cheating moonlight, but Mowgli's muscles, trained by years of experience, bore him up as though he were a feather. When a rotten log or a hidden stone turned under his foot he saved himself, never checking his pace, without effort and without thought. When he tired of ground-going he threw up his hands monkey-fashion to the nearest creeper, and seemed to float rather than to climb up into the thin branches, whence he would follow a tree-road till his mood changed, and he shot downwards in a long leafy curve to the levels again. There were still hot hollows surrounded by wet rocks where he could hardly breathe for the heavy scents of the night-flowers, and the bloom along the creeper-buds; dark avenues where the moonlight lay in belts as regular as chequered marbles in a church aisle; thickets where the wet young growth stood breast-high about him and threw its arms round his waist; and hilltops crowned with broken rock, where he leaped from stone to stone above the lairs of the frightened little foxes. He would hear, very faint and far off, the *chug-drug* of a boar sharpening his tusks on a bole; and later would come across the great brute all alone, scribing and rending the red bark of a tree, his mouth dripping with foam and his eyes blazing like fire. Or he would turn aside to the sound of clashing horns and hissing grunts and dash past a couple of furious sambur, staggering to and fro with lowered heads, striped with blood that shows black in the moonlight. Or at some rushing ford he would hear Jacala the Crocodile bellowing like a bull, or disturb a knot of the Poison-People, but before they could strike he would be away and across the glistening shingle, and deep into the jungle again.

So he ran, sometimes shouting, sometimes singing to himself, the happiest thing in all the jungle that night, till the smell of the flowers warned him that he was near the marshes, and those lay far beyond his farthest hunting-grounds.

Here, again, a man-trained man would have sunk over his head in three strides, but Mowgli's feet had eyes in them and they passed him from tussock to tussock and clump to quaking clump without asking help from the eyes in his head. He headed out to the middle of the swamp, disturbing the duck as he ran, and sat down on a moss-coated tree-trunk lapped in the black water. The marsh was awake all round him, for in the spring the Bird-People sleep very lightly, and companies of them were coming or going the night through. But no one took any notice of Mowgli sitting among the tall reeds humming songs without words and looking at the soles of his hard brown feet in case of neglected thorns. All his unhappiness seemed to have been left behind in his own jungle, and he was just beginning a song when it came back again—ten times worse than before. To make all worse the moon was setting.

This time Mowgli was frightened. "It is here also!" he said half aloud. "It has followed me," and he looked over his shoulder to see whether the It were not standing behind him. "There is no one here." The night noises in the marsh went on, but never bird or beast spoke to him, and the new feeling of misery grew.

"I have eaten poison," he said, in an awe-stricken voice. "It must be that carelessly I have eaten poison, and my strength is going from me. I was afraid—and yet it was not *I* that was afraid—Mowgli was afraid when the two wolves fought. Akela, or even Phao, would have silenced them, yet Mowgli was afraid. That is sure sign I have eaten poison. . . . But what do they care in the jungle? They sing and howl and fight, and run in companies under the moon, and I—*Hai mai!*—I am dying in the marshes, of that poison which I have eaten." He was so sorry for himself that he nearly wept. "And after," he went on, "they will find me lying in the black water. Nay, I will go back to my own jungle and I will die upon the Council Rock, and Bagheera whom I love, if he is not screaming in the valley, Bagheera, perhaps, may watch by what is left for a little, lest Chil use me as he used Akela."

A large warm tear splashed down on his knee, and, miserable as he was, Mowgli felt happy that he was so miserable, if you understand that upside-down sort of happiness. "As Chil the Kite used Akela," he repeated, "on the night I saved the pack from Red Dog." He was quiet for a little, thinking of the last words of the Lone Wolf,* which you, of course, remember. "Now Akela said to me many foolish things before he died, for when we die our stomachs change. He said . . . None the less, I *am* of the jungle!"

---

*Mortally wounded in the fight against Red Dog, Akela tells Mowgli, "Thou art a man, Little Brother," and entreats him to "Go to thine own people."

In his excitement, as he remembered the fight on Wainganga bank, he shouted the last words aloud, and a wild buffalo-cow among the reeds sprang to her knees, snorting: "Man!"

"*Uhh!*" said Mysa the Wild Buffalo (Mowgli could hear him turn in his wallow), "*that* is no man. It is only the hairless wolf of the Seeonee Pack. On such nights runs he to and fro."

"*Uhh!*" said the cow, dropping her head again to graze, "I thought it was Man."

"I say no. Oh, Mowgli, is it danger?" lowed Mysa.

"Oh, Mowgli, is it danger?" the boy called back mockingly. "That is all Mysa thinks for: Is it danger? But for Mowgli, who goes to and fro in the jungle by night watching, what care ye?"

"How loud he cries?" said the cow.

"Thus do they cry," Mysa answered contemptuously, "who having torn the grass up know not how to eat it."

"For less than this," Mowgli groaned to himself, "for less than this even last rains I had pricked Mysa out of his wallow and ridden him through the swamp on a rush halter." He stretched his hand to break one of the feathery reeds, but drew it back with a sigh. Mysa went on steadily chewing the cud and the long grass ripped where the cow grazed. "I will not die *here*," he said angrily. "Mysa, who is of one blood with Jacala and the pig, would mock me. Let us go beyond the swamp, and see what comes. Never have I run such a spring running—hot and cold together. Up, Mowgli!"

He could not resist the temptation of stealing across the reeds to Mysa and pricking him with the point of his knife. The great dripping bull broke out of his wallow like a shell exploding, while Mowgli laughed till he sat down.

"Say now that the hairless wolf of the Seeonee Pack once herded thee, Mysa," he called.

"Wolf! *Thou?*" the bull snorted, stamping in the mud. "All the jungle knows thou wast a herder of tame cattle— such a man's brat as shouts in the dust by the crops yonder. *Thou* of the jungle! What hunter would have crawled like a snake among the leeches, and for a muddy jest—a jackal's jest—have shamed me before my cow? Come to firm ground, and I will—I will . . ." Mysa frothed at the mouth, for he has nearly the worst temper of any one in the jungle.

Mowgli watched him puff and blow with eyes that never changed. When he could make himself heard through the spattering mud-shower, he said: "What man pack lair here by the marshes, Mysa? This is new jungle to me."

"Go north, then," roared the angry bull, for Mowgli had pricked him rather sharply. "It was a naked cowherd's jest. Go and tell them at the village at the foot of the marsh."

"The man pack do not love jungle-tales, nor do I think, Mysa, that a scratch more or less on thy hide is any matter for a council. But I will go and look at this village. Yes, I will go. Softly now! It is not every night that the master of the jungle comes to herd thee."

He stepped out to the shivering ground on the edge of the marsh, well knowing that Mysa would never charge over it, and laughed, as he ran, to think of the bull's anger.

"My strength is not altogether gone," he said. "It may be the poison is not to the bone. There is a star sitting low yonder." He looked at it steadily between half-shut hands. "By the bull that bought me, it is the Red Flower—the Red Flower that I lay beside before—before I came even to the first Seeonee Pack! Now that I have seen I will finish the running."

The marsh ended in a broad plain where a light twinkled. It was a long time since Mowgli had concerned himself with the doings of men, but this night the glimmer of the Red Flower drew him forward as if it had been new game.

"I will look," said he, "and I will see how far the man pack has changed."

Forgetting that he was no longer in his own jungle where he could do what he pleased, he trod carelessly through the dew-loaded grasses till he came to the hut where the light stood. Three or four yelping dogs gave tongue, for he was on the outskirts of a village.

"Ho!" said Mowgli, sitting down noiselessly, after sending back a deep wolf-growl that silenced the curs. "What comes will come. Mowgli, what hast thou to do any more with the lairs of the man pack?" He rubbed his mouth, remembering where a stone had struck it years ago when the other man pack had cast him out.

The door of the hut opened and a woman stood peering out into the darkness. A child cried, and the woman said over her shoulder: "Sleep. It was but a jackal that waked the dogs. In a little time morning comes."

Mowgli in the grass began to shake as though he had the fever. He knew that voice well, but to make sure he cried softly, surprised to find how man's talk came back: "Messua! O Messua!"

"Who calls?" said the woman, a quiver in her voice.

"Hast thou forgotten?" said Mowgli. His throat was dry as he spoke.

"If it be *thou,* what name did I give thee? Say!" She had half shut the door, and her hand was clutching at her breast.

"Nathoo! Ohé Nathoo!" said Mowgli, for, as you know, that was the name Messua gave him when he first came to the man pack.

"Come, my son," she called, and Mowgli stepped into the light, and looked full at Messua, the woman who had been good to him, and whose life he had saved from the man pack so long before. She was older, and her hair was grey, but her eyes and her voice had not changed. Woman-like, she expected to find Mowgli where she had left him, and her eyes travelled upwards in a puzzled fashion from his chest to his head, that touched the top of the door.

"My son," she stammered, and then sinking to his feet: "But it is no longer my son. It is a godling of the woods! *Ahai!*"

As he stood in the red light of the oil-lamp, strong, tall, and beautiful, his long black hair sweeping over his shoulders, the knife swinging at his neck, and his head crowned with a wreath of white jasmine, he might easily have been mistaken for some wild god of a jungle legend. The child half asleep on a cot sprang up and shrieked aloud with terror. Messua turned to soothe him while Mowgli stood still, looking in at the water-jars and cooking-pots, the grain-bin and all the other human belongings that he found himself remembering so well.

"What wilt thou eat or drink?" Messua murmured. "This is all thine. We owe our lives to thee. But art thou him I called Nathoo, or a godling, indeed?"

"I am Nathoo," said Mowgli, "I am very far from my own place. I saw this light and came hither. I did not know thou wast here."

"After we came to Khanhiwara," Messua said timidly, "the English would have helped us against those villagers that sought to burn us. Rememberest thou?"

"Indeed, I have not forgotten."

"But when the English Law was made ready we went to the village of those evil people and it was no more to be found."

"That also I remember," said Mowgli, with a quiver of the nostril.

"My man, therefore, took service in the fields, and at last, for indeed he was a strong man, we held a little land here. It is not so rich as the old village, but we do not need much—we two."

"Where is he—the man that dug in the dirt when he was afraid on that night?"

"He is dead—a year."

"And he?" Mowgli pointed to the child.

"My son that was born two rains ago. If thou art a godling give him the favour of the jungle that he may be safe among thy—thy people as we were safe on that night."

She lifted up the child, who, forgetting his fright, reached out to play with the knife that hung on Mowgli's chest, and Mowgli put the little fingers aside very carefully.

"And if thou art Nathoo whom the tigers carried away," Messua went on choking, "he is then thy younger brother. Give him an elder brother's blessing."

"*Hai mai!* What do I know of the thing called a blessing? I am neither a godling nor his brother, and—O Mother, Mother, my heart is heavy in me." He shivered as he set down the child.

"Like enough," said Messua, bustling among the cooking-pots. "This comes of running about the marshes by night. Beyond question, a fever has soaked thee to the marrow." Mowgli smiled a little at the idea of anything in the jungle hurting him. "I will make a fire and thou shalt drink warm milk. Put away the jasmine wreath, the smell is heavy in so small a place."

Mowgli sat down, muttering, his face in his hands. All manner of strange feelings were running over him, exactly as though he had been poisoned, and he felt dizzy and a little sick. He drank the warm milk in long gulps, Messua patting him on the shoulder from time to time, not quite sure whether he were her son Nathoo of the long-ago days or some wonderful jungle being, but glad to feel that he was at least flesh and blood.

"Son," she said at last. Her eyes were full of pride. "Have any told thee that thou art beautiful beyond all men?"

"Hah?" said Mowgli, for of course he had never heard

anything of the kind. Messua laughed softly and happily. The look in his face was enough for her.

"I am the first, then? It is right, though it comes seldom, that a mother should tell her son these good things. Thou art very beautiful. Never have I looked upon such a man."

Mowgli twisted his head and tried to see over his own hard shoulder, and Messua laughed again so long that Mowgli, not knowing why, was forced to laugh with her, and the child ran from one to the other laughing too.

"Nay, thou must not mock thy brother," said Messua catching him to her breast. "When thou art one-half as fair we will marry thee to the youngest daughter of a king and thou shalt ride great elephants."

Mowgli could not understand one word in three of the talk here; the warm milk was taking effect on him after his forty-mile run; so he curled up and in a minute was deep asleep, and Messua put the hair back from his eyes, threw a cloth over him and was happy. Jungle-fashion, he slept out the rest of that night and all the next day, for his instincts, which never wholly slept, warned him there was nothing to fear. He waked at last with a bound that shook the hut, for the cloth over his face made him dream of traps, and there he stood, his hand on his knife, the sleep all heavy in his rolling eyes, ready for any fight.

Messua laughed and set the evening meal before him. There were only a few coarse cakes baked over the smoky fire, some rice, and a lump of sour preserved tamarinds— just enough to go on with till he could get to his evening kill. The smell of the dew in the marshes made him hungry and restless. He wanted to finish his spring running, but the child insisted on sitting in his arms, and Messua would have it that his long blue-black hair must be combed out. So she sang as she combed, foolish little baby songs, now calling Mowgli her son, and now begging him to give some of his jungle-power to the child. The hut door was closed, but Mowgli heard a sound he knew well, and saw Messua's jaw drop with horror as a great grey paw came under the bottom of the door, and Grey Brother outside whined a muffled and penitent whine of anxiety and fear.

"Out and wait. Ye would not come when I called," said Mowgli in jungle-talk, never turning his head, and the great grey paw disappeared.

"Do not—do not bring thy—thy servants with thee," said Messua. "I—we have always lived at peace with the jungle."

"It is peace," said Mowgli, rising. "Think of that night on the road to Khanhiwara. There were scores of such folk before thee and behind thee. But I see that even in spring-time the Jungle-People do not always forget. Mother, I go."

Messua drew aside humbly—he was indeed a wood-god she thought—but as his hand was on the door the mother in her made her throw her arms round Mowgli's neck again and again.

"Come back!" she whispered. "Son or no son, come back, for I love thee—and look, he too grieves."

The child was crying because the man with the shiny knife was going away.

"Come back again," Messua repeated. "By night or by

day this door is never shut to thee."

Mowgli's throat worked as though the cords in it were being pulled, and his voice seemed to be dragged from it as he answered: "I will surely come back."

"And now," he said, as he put aside the head of the fawning wolf on the threshold, "I have a little cry against thee, Grey Brother. Why came ye not, all Four, when I called so long ago?"

"So long ago? It was but last night. I—we—were singing in the jungle, the new songs, for this is the Time of New Talk. Rememberest thou?"

"Truly, truly."

"And as soon as the songs were sung," Grey Brother went on earnestly, "I followed thy trail. I ran from all the others and followed hot-foot. But, O Little Brother, what hast *thou* done—eating and sleeping with the man pack?"

"If ye had come when I called this had never been," said Mowgli, running much faster.

"And now what is to be?" said Grey Brother.

Mowgli was going to answer when a girl in a white cloth came down some path that led from the outskirts of the village. Grey Brother dropped out of sight at once and Mowgli backed noiselessly into a field of high-springing crops. He could almost have touched her with his hand when the warm green stalks closed before his face and he disappeared like a ghost. The girl screamed, for she thought she had seen a spirit, and then she gave a deep sigh. Mowgli parted the stalks with his hands and watched her till she was out of sight.

"And now I do not know," he said, sighing in his turn. *"Why* did ye not come when I called?"

"We follow thee—we follow thee," Grey Brother mumbled, licking at Mowgli's heel. "We follow thee always except in the Time of the New Talk."

"And would ye follow me to the man pack?" Mowgli whispered.

"Did I not follow thee on the night that our old pack cast thee out? Who waked thee lying among the crops?"

"Aye, but again?"

"Have I not followed thee to-night?"

"Aye, but again and again, and it may be again, Grey Brother?"

Grey Brother was silent. When he spoke he growled to himself: "The Black One spoke truth."

"And he said?"

"Man goes to Man at the last. Raksha our mother said—"

"So also said Akela on the night of Red Dog," Mowgli muttered.

"So also said Kaa, who is wiser than us all."

"What dost thou say, Grey Brother?"

"They cast thee out once, with bad talk. They cut thy mouth with stones. They sent Buldeo to slay thee. They would have thrown thee into the Red Flower. Thou, and not I, hast said that they are evil and senseless. Thou and not I—I follow my own people—didst let in the jungle upon them. Thou and not I didst make song against them more bitter even than our song against Red Dog."

"I ask thee what *thou* sayest?"

They were talking as they ran. Grey Brother cantered on a while without replying, and then he said between bound and bound as it were: "Man-cub—master of the jungle—son of Raksha—lair-brother to me—though I forget for a little while in the spring, thy trail is my trail, thy lair is my lair, thy kill is my kill, and thy death-fight is my death-fight. I speak for the Three. But what wilt thou say to the jungle?"

"That is well thought. Between the sight and the kill it is not good to wait. Go before and cry them all to the Council Rock, and I will tell them what is in my stomach. But they may not come—in the Time of the New Talk they may forget me."

"Hast thou then forgotten nothing?" snapped Grey Brother over his shoulder, as he laid himself down to gallop, and Mowgli followed, thinking.

At any other season his news would have called all the jungle together with bristling necks, but now they were busy hunting and fighting and killing and singing. From one to another Grey Brother ran, crying: "The master of the jungle goes back to Man. Come to the Council Rock!" And the happy, eager people only answered: "He will return in the summer heats. The rains will drive him to lair. Run and sing with us, Grey Brother."

"But the master of the jungle goes back to Man," Grey Brother would repeat.

"*Eee—Yowa?* Is the Time of New Talk any less good for that?" they would reply. So when Mowgli, heavyhearted, came up through the well-remembered rocks to the place where he had been brought into the pack, he found only the Four, Baloo, who was nearly blind with age, and the heavy, cold-blooded Kaa, coiled round Akela's empty seat.

"Thy trail ends here, then, manling?" said Kaa, as Mowgli threw himself down, his face in his hands. "Cry thy cry. We be of one blood, thou and I—man and snake together."

"Why was I not torn in two by Red Dog?" the boy moaned. "My strength is gone from me, and it is not the poison. By night and by day I hear a double step upon my trail. When I turn my head it is as though one had hidden himself from me that instant. I go to look behind the trees and he is not there. I call and none cry again, but it is as though one listened and kept back the answer. I lie down, but I do not rest. I run the spring running, but I am not made still. I bathe, but I am not made cool. The kill sickens me, but I have no heart to fight except I kill. The Red Flower is in my body, my bones are water—and—I know not what I know."

"What need of talk?" said Baloo, slowly, turning his head to where Mowgli lay. "Akela by the river said it, that Mowgli should drive Mowgli back to the man pack. I said it. But who listens now to Baloo? Bagheera—where is Bagheera this night? He knows also. It is the Law."

"When we met at the Cold Lairs, manling, I knew it," said Kaa, turning a little in his mighty coils. "Man goes to Man at the last, though the jungle does not cast him out."

The Four looked at one another and at Mowgli, puzzled but obedient.

"The jungle does not cast me out, then?" Mowgli stammered.

Grey Brother and the Three growled furiously, beginning: "So long as we live none shall dare—" But Baloo checked them.

"I taught thee the Law. It is for me to speak," he said, "and though I cannot now see the rocks before me, I see far. Little frog, take thine own trail; make thy lair with thine own blood and pack and people; but when there is need of foot or tooth or eye or a word carried swiftly by night, remember, master of the jungle, the jungle is thine at call."

"The Middle Jungle is thine also," said Kaa. "I speak for no small people."

"*Hai mai,* my brothers," cried Mowgli, throwing up his arms with a sob. "I know not what I know, I would not go, but I am drawn by both feet. How shall I leave these nights?"

"Nay, look up, Little Brother," Baloo repeated. "There is no shame in this hunting. When the honey is eaten we leave the empty hive."

"Having cast the skin," said Kaa, "we may not creep into it afresh. It is the Law."

"Listen, dearest of all to me," said Baloo. "There is neither word nor will here to hold thee back. Look up! Who may question the master of the jungle? I saw thee playing among the white pebbles yonder when thou wast a little frog; and Bagheera, that bought thee for the price of a young bull newly killed, saw thee also. Of that looking-over we two only remain, for Raksha, thy lair-mother, is dead with thy lair-father; the old wolf pack is long since dead; thou knowest whither Shere Khan went, and Akela died among the dholes, where but for thy wisdom and strength the second Seeonee Pack would also have died. There remain nothing but old bones. It is no longer the man-cub that asks leave of his pack, but the master of the jungle that changes his trail. Who shall question man in his ways?"

"But Bagheera and the bull that bought me," said Mowgli. "I would not—"

His words were cut short by a roar and a crash in the thicket below, and Bagheera, light, strong, and terrible as always.

"Therefore," he said, stretching out a dripping right paw, "I did not come. It was a long hunt, but he lies dead in the bushes now—a bull in his second year—the bull that frees thee, Little Brother. All debts are paid now. For the rest, my word is Baloo's word." He licked Mowgli's foot. "Remember Bagheera loved thee," he cried and bounded away. At the foot of the hill he cried again long and loud: "Good hunting on a new trail, master of the jungle! Remember Bagheera loved thee."

"Thou hast heard," said Baloo. "There is no more. Go now, but first come to me. O wise little frog, come to me!"

"It is hard to cast the skin," said Kaa, as Mowgli sobbed and sobbed with his head on the blind bear's side and his arms round his neck, while Baloo tried feebly to lick his feet.

"The stars are thin," said Grey Brother, snuffing at the dawn-wind. "Where shall we lair to-day? For, from now, we follow new trails."

And this is the last of the Mowgli stories.

THE OUTSONG

This Is the Song That Mowgli Heard Behind Him in the
Jungle Till He Came to Messua's Door Again.

BALOO

For the sake of him who showed
One wise frog the jungle-road,
Keep the Law the man pack make—
For thy blind old Baloo's sake!
Clean or tainted, hot or stale,
Hold it as it were the trail,
Through the day and through the night,
Questing neither left nor right.
For the sake of him who loves
Thee beyond all else that moves,
When thy pack would make thee pain,
Say: "Tabaqui sings again."
When thy pack would work thee ill,
Say: "Shere Khan is yet to kill."
When the knife is drawn to slay,
Keep the Law and go thy way.
(Root and honey, palm and spathe,
Guard a cub from harm and scathe.)
Wood and water, wind and tree,
Jungle-favour go with thee!

KAA

Anger is the egg of fear—
Only lidless eyes are clear.
Cobra-poison none may leech;
Even so with cobra-speech.
Open talk shall call to thee
Strength whose mate is courtesy.
Send no lunge beyond thy length;
Lend no rotten bough thy strength.
Gauge thy gape with buck or goat,
Lest thine eye should choke thy throat.
After gorging, wouldst thou sleep?
Look thy den is hid and deep,
Lest a wrong, by thee forgot,
Draw thy killer to the spot.
East and West and North and South,
Wash thy skin and close thy mouth.
(Pit and rift and blue pool-brim
Middle Jungle follow him!)
Wood and water, wind and tree,
Jungle-favour go with thee!

BAGHEERA

In the cage my life began;
Well I know the ways of Man.
By the broken lock that freed—
Man-cub 'ware the man-cub's breed!
Scenting-dew or starlight pale,
Choose no idle tree-cat trail.
Pack or council, hunt or den,
Cry no truce with Jackal-Men.
Feed them silence when they say:
"Come with us an easy way."
Feed them silence when they seek
Help of thine to hurt the weak.
Make no *bandar's* boast of skill;
Hold thy peace above the kill.
Let not call nor song nor sign
Turn thee from thy hunting-line.
(Morning mist or twilight clear
Serve him, wardens of the deer!)
Wood and water, wind and tree,
Jungle-favour go with thee!

THE THREE

On the trail that thou must tread
To the threshold of our dread,
Where the flower blossoms red;
Through the nights when thou shalt lie
Prisoned from our mother-sky,
Hearing us, thy loves, go by;
In the dawns, when thou shalt wake
To the toil thou canst not break,
Heartsick for the jungle's sake;
Wood and water, wind and tree,
Jungle-favour go with thee!

Interpretive Questions

1. Why is Mowgli, who has always delighted in the turn of the seasons, overcome by pure unhappiness during this Time of New Talk? (114)

2. Why is it the Law that "Mowgli should drive Mowgli back to the man pack," and not that the jungle should cast him out? (132)

3. Why is Mowgli able to be part of the jungle only when he is a child, and not when he becomes a man?

ERNAL CONFLICT PLOT AND
PLOT AND INTERNAL CONFL
L CONFLICT PLOT AND INTE
T AND INT   CONFLICT
CONFLICT P   ND INTERN
AND INTER   ONFLICT P
ON   TERN
ND I **Thinking** PLO
Interpretively
ICT PLOT AND INTERNAL C
ERNAL CONFLICT PLOT AND
PLOT AND INTERNAL CONFL
L CONFLICT PLOT AND INTE
T AND INTERNAL CONF
CONFLICT PLOT AND INT
AND INTERNAL CONELL
CONFLICT PLOT / **Thin**
ND INTERNAL CO
NFLICT PLOT **Interpr**
INTERNAL CC
ICT PLOT AND INTERNAL C
ERNAL CONFLICT PLOT AND
PLOT AND INTERNAL CONFL
L CONFLICT PLOT AND INTE
T AND INTERNAL CONFLICT
CONFLICT PLOT AND INTERN
AND I   NAL CONFLICT P
CONFL   OT AND INTERN
ND INT   CONFLICT PLO
                INTERNA
Thinking T PLOT A
                AL C
terpretively AND
LOT AND INTERNAL CONFL
L CONFLICT PLOT AND INTE
T AND INTERNAL CO
CONFLICT PLOT AND I
AND INTERNAL CON
CONFLICT PLO   **Thinki**
ID INTERNAL
NFLICT PLC **Interpret**
INTERNAL (
ICT PLOT AND INTERNAL C
RNAL CONFLICT PLOT AND
L   D INTERNAL CONFL
       ICT PLOT AND INTE
                AL CONFLICT
inking AND INTERN
                CONFLICT P
rpretively D INTERN
                LICT PLO
NFLICT PLOT AND INTERNA
NTERNAL CONFLICT PLOT A
ICT PLOT AND INTERNAL C
RNAL CONFLICT P   ND
PLOT AND INTERN   NFL
L CONFLICT PLOT   TE
T AND INT
ONFLICT PI **Thinkin**
AND IN   **Interpretiv**
CONFLIC
ID INTERNAL CONFLICT PLO
NFLICT PLOT AND INTERNA
NTERNAL CONFLICT PLOT A
ICT PLOT AND INTERNAL C
RNAL   ICT PLOT AND
LOT A   ERNAL CONFL
          ND INTE
Thinking ONFLICT
                ERN
terpretively CT P

Thinking Interpretively: Plot and Internal Conflict

Some stories, such as "Letting in the Jungle," describe a character in conflict with others. However, in "The Spring Running," the problem or conflict to be resolved is primarily internal—one that Mowgli feels within himself. In order to fully understand any story whose plot centers around a character's internal conflict, we must have an especially clear idea of how the character's feelings change over the course of the story. There are some basic, general questions we can ask that will help us do this. Let us try asking these questions about "The Spring Running."

What is the character's inner problem or conflict?

Very early in "The Spring Running," we learn that Mowgli is unhappy. How do we know this? We can see his "bad temper" in the way that he's acting—and in the "bad talk" that he gives his friend Bagheera. Also, the author tells us directly that up to this year Mowgli "had always delighted in the turn of the seasons," but that now when he opened his mouth to join in the announcement of spring, "the words choked between his teeth, and a feeling came over him that began at his toes and ended in his hair—a feeling of pure unhappiness" (p. 114).

But *why* is Mowgli so unhappy? The author does not tell us. Instead, we must discover the answer for ourselves, following along as Mowgli tries to lose his unhappiness during his spring running, only to have it return "ten times worse than before" when he stops near the faraway marshes.

Gradually, it becomes clear to us that Mowgli is in

conflict about leaving the jungle. In describing his feelings of confusion to Kaa, Mowgli even talks about himself as if he were two different people: "By night and by day I hear a double step upon my trail. When I turn my head it is as though one had hidden himself from me that instant. . . . I know not what I know" (p. 132). It is Mowgli's deep, mixed feelings about where he belongs that are the source of his unhappiness.

Does the character make any important decisions or come to any important realizations?

One turning point in "The Spring Running" occurs when Mowgli, having finished his run, decides to go to what turns out to be Messua's village. Another is when Mowgli—realizing the strength of his bond to Man—promises Messua that he will "surely come back" to her again. Being alert to what Mowgli says and feels when facing these decisions brings us closer to the turmoil he is experiencing. *Why,* for example, *does Mowgli blame his visit to Messua's village on Grey Brother? Why does he say "If ye had come when I called this had never been"?*

Realizing the depth of Mowgli's inner conflict about leaving the jungle can also help us rethink earlier events in the story that are puzzling, such as Mowgli's anger when he comes across the two young wolves of the pack fighting. *Why does Mowgli's unhappiness tempt him to kill the fighting wolves, even though they are obeying the Law of the Jungle?*

How is the character's inner problem or conflict resolved?

At the end of a story in which an internal problem is described, the character's conflict may not be completely settled. Nevertheless, we can usually identify some kind of significant change that has occurred. One way to do this is by comparing what the character is like at the beginning of the story with what he or she is like at the end. For instance, "The Spring Running" opens with Mowgli unhappy and unable to say why he is so miserable. At the story's conclusion, Mowgli cannot entirely explain his need to leave the jungle, but he at least knows he must. He is still sad, but it is a different kind of sadness. Drawing such comparisons prepares us to reflect further on why, at the end of the story, it is easier for the Free Hunters to accept Mowgli's leaving than it is for Mowgli. *Why does Mowgli throw up his arms "with a sob" and say "I know not what I know, I would not go, but I am drawn by both feet"?*

Thinking interpretively about the changes Mowgli undergoes over the course of the story helps us to sympathize with his confusion. This, in turn, allows us to think more accurately about what the story means—to draw our own conclusions about why, as Baloo says, it is the Law that "Mowgli should drive Mowgli back to the man pack." Ultimately, looking closely at the plot in this way can help us understand why Mowgli is able to be a part of the jungle only while he is a child, and not once he becomes a man. ▮▮

This story takes place in Israel in the mid-1940s, just before independence. Palestine, as it was then called, had a mixed population of native Arabs and Jewish immigrants from all over Europe. It had been controlled by Great Britain since the end of World War I. With the coming of World War II, Britain, hoping to keep Arab good will, began restricting further Jewish immigration and settlement in the area. Increasing tension between the British government and the Jewish Underground was finally resolved when the independent state of Israel was proclaimed on May 14, 1948.

Soumchi

Amos Oz

PROLOGUE
On Changes

In which may be found a variety of memories and reflections, comparisons and conclusions. You may skip them if you'd rather and pass straight on to Chapter One where my story proper begins.

Everything changes. My friends and acquaintances, for example, change curtains and professions, exchange old homes for new ones, shares for securities, or vice versa, bicycles for motor bicycles, motor bicycles for cars, exchange stamps, coins, letters, good mornings, ideas and opinions: some of them exchange smiles.

In the part of Jerusalem known as Sha'are Hesed there once lived a bank cashier who, in the course of a single month, changed his home, his wife, his appearance (he grew a red moustache and sideburns—also reddish),

145

changed first name and surname, changed sleeping and eating habits; in short, he changed everything. One fine day he even changed his job, became a drummer in a night club instead of a cashier (though actually this was not so much a case of change, more like a sock being turned inside out).

Even while we are reflecting on it, by the way, the world about us is gradually changing too. Though the blue transparency of summer still lies across the land, though it is still hot and the sky still blazes above our heads, yet already, near dusk, you can sense some new coolness—at night comes a breeze and the smell of clouds. And just as the leaves begin to redden and to turn, so the sea becomes a little more blue, the earth a little more brown, even the far-off hills these days look somewhat further away.

Everything.

As for me; aged eleven and two months, approximately, I changed completely, four or five times, in the course of a single day. How then shall I begin my story? With Uncle Zemach or Esthie? Either would do. But I think I'll begin with Esthie.

1

In Which Love Blossoms

And in which facts will at last be revealed that have been kept secret to this day; love and other feelings among them.

Near us in Zachariah Street lived a girl called Esthie. I loved her. In the morning, sitting at the breakfast table and eating a slice of bread, I'd whisper to myself, "Esthie."

To which my father would return: "One doesn't eat with one's mouth open."

While, in the evenings, they'd say of me: "That crazy boy has shut himself in the bathroom again and is playing with water."

Only I was not playing with water at all, merely filling up the hand basin and tracing her name with my finger across the waves on its surface. At night sometimes I dreamed that Esthie was pointing at me in the street, shouting, "Thief, thief!" And I would be frightened and begin to run away and she would pursue me; everyone would pursue me, Bar-Kochba Sochobolski and Goel Germanski and Aldo and Elie Weingarten, everyone, the pursuit continuing across empty lots and backyards, over fences and heaps of rusty junk, among ruins and down alleyways, until my pursuers began to grow tired and gradually to lag behind, and at last only Esthie and I would be left running all alone, reaching almost together some remote and distant spot, a woodshed, perhaps, or a washhouse on a roof, or the dark angle under the stairs of a strange house, and then the dream would become both sweet and terrible—oh, I'd awake at night sometimes and weep, almost, from shame. I wrote two love poems in the black notebook that I lost in the Tel Arza wood. Perhaps it was a good thing I lost it.

But what did Esthie know?

Esthie knew nothing. Or knew and wondered.

For example: once I put my hand up in a geography lesson and stated authoritatively:

"Lake Hula is also known as Lake Soumchi." The whole classroom of course immediately roared with loud and unruly laughter. What I had said was the truth; the exact truth in fact, it's in the encyclopedia. In spite of which, our teacher, Mr. Shitrit, got confused for a moment and interrogated me furiously: "Kindly sum up the evidence by which you support your conclusion." But the class had already erupted, was shouting and screaming from every direction:

"Sum it up, Soumchi, sum it up, Soumchi." While Mr. Shitrit swelled like a frog, grew red in the face and roared as usual:

"Let all flesh be silent!" And then, besides: "Not a dog shall bark!"

After five more minutes the class had quieted down again. But, almost to the end of the eighth grade, I remained Soumchi. I've no ulterior motive in telling you all this. I simply want to stress one significant detail; a note sent to me by Esthie at the end of that same lesson, which read as follows:

You're nuts. Why do you always have to say things that get you into trouble? Stop it!

Only then she had folded over one corner at the bottom of the note and written in it, very small: *But it doesn't matter. E.*

So what did Esthie know?

Esthie knew nothing, or perhaps she knew and wondered. As for me, in no circumstance would it have occurred to me to hide a love letter in her satchel as Elie Weingarten did in Nourit's, nor to send her a message via Ra'anana, our class matchmaker, like Tarzan Bamberger, also to Nourit. Quite the reverse: this is what I did; on every possible occasion I'd pull Esthie's plaits; time and again I stuck her beautiful white jumper to her chair with chewing gum.

Why did I do it? Because. Why not? To show her. And I'd twist her two thin arms behind her back nearly as hard as I could, until she started calling me names and scratching me, yet she never begged for mercy. That's what I did to Esthie. And worse besides. It was me who first nicknamed her Clementine (from the song that the English soldiers at the Schneller Barracks were spreading round Jerusalem those days: *"Oh my darling, oh my darling, oh my dar-ling Clementine!"*—the girls in our class, surprisingly, picked it up quite gleefully, and even at Hanukah six months later, when everything was over, they were still calling Esthie Tina, which came from Clementina, which came from Clementine).

And Esthie? She only had one word for me and she

threw it in my face first thing every morning, before I had even had time to start making a nuisance of myself:

"Louse"—or else:

"You stink."

Once or twice at the ten o'clock break I very nearly reduced Esthie to tears. For that I was handed punishments by Hemda, our teacher, and took them like a man, tight-lipped and uncomplaining.

And that's how love blossomed, without notable event, until the day after the feast of Shavuot. Esthie wept on my account at the ten o'clock break and I wept on hers at night.

2

With All His Heart and Soul

In which Uncle Zemach goes too far and I set out for the source of the River Zambezi (in the heart of Africa).

At the feast of Shavuot, Uncle Zemach came from Tel Aviv, bringing me a bicycle as a present. As a matter of fact my birthday falls between the two festivals—of Passover and Shavuot. But in Uncle Zemach's eyes, all festivals are more or less the same, except for the Tree Planting festival which he treats with exceptional respect. He used to say, "At Hanukah we children of Israel are taught in school to be angry with the wicked Greeks. At Purim it's the Persians; at Passover we hate Egypt, at Lag B'omer, Rome. On May Day we demonstrate against England; on the Ninth of Av we fast against Babylon and Rome; on the twentieth of

Tammuz, Herzl and Bialik died, while on the eleventh of
Adar we must remember for all eternity what the Arabs did
to Trumpedor and his companions at Tel Hai. The Tree
Planting festival is the only one where we haven't quar-
reled with anyone and have no griefs to remember. But it
almost always rains then—it does it on purpose."

My Uncle Zemach, they had explained to me, was
Grandmother Emilia's eldest son by her first marriage, before she married Grandfather Isidore. Sometimes, when he
was staying with us, Uncle Zemach would get me out of
bed at half past five in the morning and incite me in a whisper to steal into the kitchen with him and cook ourselves an
illicit double omelette. He would have a cheerful, even
wicked gleam in his eye on those mornings, behaving just
as if he and I were fellow members of some dangerous gang
and only temporarily engaged in such a relatively innocent
pastime as cooking ourselves illicit double omelettes. But
my family generally had a very low opinion of my Uncle
Zemach. Like this for instance:

"He was a little *spekulant** by the time he was fourteen
in Warsaw, in the Nalevki district, and now here he is, still
a *spekulant* in Bugrashov Street in Tel Aviv." Or:

"He hasn't changed an atom. Even the sun can't be bothered to brown him. That's the type he is. And there's nothing whatever we can do about it."

But I regarded that last remark as plain stupid and nasty,
as well as unfair. My Uncle Zemach didn't get brown because he couldn't and that was all there was to it. Even if

---

spekulant. Black marketeer.—TRANS.

they'd made him a lifeguard on the beach he'd have got burnt instead of brown, turned red all over and begun to peel. This is how he was; a young man still, not tall, and so thin and pale he might have been cut out of paper. His hair was whitish, his eyes red like a rabbit's.

And what did *spekulant* mean anyway? I had no idea at all. But in my own mind translated it more or less as follows:

That even when he lived in Warsaw, Uncle Zemach had used to wear a vest and khaki shorts down to his knees and fall fast asleep with the radio on. And he still had not changed; he still clung to his outlandish habits, wore a vest and khaki shorts down to his knees and fell asleep with the radio on. Even here, in Palestine, in Bugrashov Street, Tel Aviv. Well, I thought, what about it, so what?—what's wrong with that? And anyway, my Uncle Zemach lived in Grusenberg Street, not Bugrashov Street. And anyway, sometimes he would burst out singing very loudly in a voice that mooed and brayed and broke,

"Oh, show me the way to go home . . ."

At which they would whisper together, very worried and in Yiddish so that I wouldn't understand, but always with the word *meshuggener,* which I knew meant madman. But though they said this of Uncle Zemach, he struck me rather—when he burst out with this song or any other—as not at all a mad man, but simply very sad.

And sometimes he wasn't sad either. Not at all: quite the reverse, he'd be joyous and funny. For instance, he would sit with my parents and my unmarried Aunt Edna on our balcony at dusk and discuss matters which ought not under any circumstances to have been discussed in front of children.

Bargains and profits, building lots and swindles, shares and *lirot,** scandals and adulteries in Bohemian circles. Sometimes, until they silenced him furiously, he used dirty language. "Quiet, Wetmark," they would say, "what's the matter with you, are you crazy, have you gone completely out of your mind? The boy's listening to everything and he's no baby any more."

And the presents he would bring me. He kept on thinking up the most amazing, even outrageous, presents. Once, he brought me a Chinese stamp album that twittered when you opened it. Once, a game like Monopoly, only in Turkish. Once, a black pistol that squirted water in your enemy's face. And once he brought me a little aquarium with a pair of live fish swimming about in it, except they were not a pair, as it turned out, but both indubitably male. Another time, he brought me a dart gun. ("Are you out of your mind, Wetmark? The boy's going to put someone's eye out with that thing, God forbid.") And one winter weekend I got from Uncle Zemach a Nazi bank note—no other boy in our neighborhood had anything like it. ("Now, Wetmark, this time you have really gone too far.") And, on Seder night, he presented me with six white mice in a cage. ("So what else are you going to bring the boy? Snakes? Bedbugs? Cockroaches, perhaps?")

This time, Uncle Zemach marked the feast of Shavuot

---
*lirot. Pounds.—TRANS.

by riding all the way from the Egged bus station in the Jaffa Road to the courtyard of our house on a secondhand Raleigh bicycle, complete with every accessory: it had a bell, also a lamp, also a carrier, also a reflector at the back; all it lacked was the crossbar joining the saddle to the handlebars. But, in my first overwhelming joy, I overlooked just how grave a shortcoming that was.

Mother said: "Really, this is excessive, Zemach. The boy is still only eleven. What are you proposing to give him for his Bar Mitzva?"

"A camel," said Uncle Zemach at once, and with an air of such total indifference, he might have prepared himself for this very question all along.

Father said: "Would it be worth your considering at least once the effects on his education? Seriously, Zemach, where's it all leading to?"

I did not wait for Uncle Zemach's reply. Nor did it matter to me in the least where things were leading. Crazy with pride and joy, I was galloping my bicycle to my private place behind the house. And there, where no one could see me, I kissed its handlebars, then kissed the back of my own hands again and again and, in a whisper as loud as a shout, chanted: "Lord God Almighty, Lord God Almighty, LORD GOD ALMIGHTY." And, afterwards, in a deep, wild groan that broke from the depths of my being: "HI—MA—LA—YA."

And after that, I leaned the bicycle against a tree and leaped high into the air. It was only when I calmed down a little that I noticed Father. He stood in a window above my head and watched in unbroken silence until I had quite finished. Then he said:

"All right. So be it. All I beg is that we should make a little agreement between us. You may ride your new bicycle for up to an hour and a half each day. No more. You'll ride always on the right-hand side, whether there is traffic in the street or not. And you will remain always, exclusively, within the boundaries set by the following streets: Malachi, Zephania, Zachariah, Ovadia and Amos. You will not enter Geula Street, because it is too full of the comings and goings of the British drivers from the Schneller Barracks; whether they are intoxicated or the enemies of Israel, or both, is immaterial. And at all intersections you will kindly, please, use your intelligence a little."

"On the wings of eagles," said Uncle Zemach.

And Mother added: "Yes, but carefully."

I said: "Fine, goodbye." But when I had gone a little way from them, added: "It will be all right." And went out into the street.

How they stared at me then, the boys of our neighborhood; classmates, big boys, little boys alike. I watched them too, but sideways, so that they wouldn't notice it, and saw envy, mockery and malice there. But what did I care? Very slowly and deliberately I processed in front of them, not riding my bicycle, but pushing it, one-handed, along the pavement, right under their noses, wearing on my face meanwhile a thoughtful, even smug, expression, as if to ask:

"What's all the fuss about? It's just a Raleigh bicycle. Of

course you can do exactly as you like. You can burst on the spot if you like, but it's your own look out. It's got absolutely nothing to do with me."

Indeed, Elie Weingarten could not keep silence any longer. He opened his mouth and said, very coolly, like a scientist identifying some unusual lizard just discovered in a field:

"Just look at this. They've gone and bought Soumchi a girl's bike, without a crossbar."

"Perhaps they'll buy him a party frock next," said Bar-Kochba Sochobolski. He did not even bother to look at me, nor cease tossing deftly up and down two silver coins at once.

"A pink hair ribbon would suit Soumchi very well,"—this was the voice of Tarzan Bamberger. "And he and Esthie can be best friends." (Bar-Kochba again.) "Except Esthie wears a bra already and Soumchi doesn't need one yet." (Elie Weingarten, the skunk.)

That was it. Enough, I decided. More than enough. Finish.

I did not start calling them names nor set about breaking their bones one by one. Instead I made them the same rude gesture with my left thumb that Uncle Zemach made whenever the name of the British Foreign Minister, Bevin,* was mentioned, turned around instantly and rode off on my bicycle down Zephania Street.

---

*Ernest Bevin, foreign minister 1945-1951, opposed the establishment of an independent Jewish state in Palestine.

Let them say anything they liked.

Let them burst in a million pieces.

What should I care?

Besides, on principle, I never pick a fight with boys weaker than myself. And, besides, what was all this about Esthie suddenly? What made them think of Esthie? Right then. It was still daylight. I would set off here and now on my bicycle for faraway places, head south on the Katamon and Talpiot Road, and on farther, via Bethlehem, Hebron and Beersheva, via the Negev and Sinai deserts, towards the heart of Africa and the source of the River Zambezi, there to brave alone a mob of bloodthirsty savages.

But I had barely reached the end of Zephania Street when I began to ask myself: Why do they hate me so, those bastards? And knew, suddenly, in my heart of hearts that it was my fault just as much as theirs. I felt an instant sense of relief. After all, an ability to show mercy even to his worst enemy is the mark of a great and noble soul. No power in all the world, no possible obstacle could deter such a man from traveling to the farthest frontiers of unknown lands. I would go now to consult Aldo, I decided, and afterwards, this very day and without more ado, would continue on my journey to Africa.

3

*Who Shall Ascend
unto the Hill of the Lord?*

*In which negotiations are concluded, a contract signed
and a number of plans discussed, as are faraway places
where no white man has ever set foot.*

In the last house but one in Zephania Street lived my
friend, Aldo Castelnuovo, whose father was famous for his
conjuring tricks with matches and playing cards; besides
which he owned a large travel agency, *The Orient Express.*
I knew that Aldo, of all people, must see my new bicycle.
It was the one thing his parents had not bought him,
though they had bought him almost everything else. They
would not allow Aldo a bicycle because of the various dan-
gers involved and, in particular, because it might hinder
Aldo's progress on the violin. It was for this reason that I
whistled to Aldo furtively, from outside his house. When
Aldo appeared he took the situation in at a glance, manag-
ing to smuggle the bicycle quickly into a disused shed in
their back garden without his mother having suspected
anything at all.

Afterwards, we both went into the house and shut ourselves up in Aldo's father's library (Professore Emilio
Castelnuovo having gone to Cairo for four days on business). It greeted me, as usual, with a smell both gloomy and
enticing, made up of muttered secrets and hushed carpets,

stealthy plots and leather upholstery, illicit whisperings and distant journeys. All day long, all summer long, the library shutters were kept closed to prevent sunlight fading the beautiful leather bindings with their gold-lettered spines.

We took out the huge German atlas and compared carefully every possible route on the map of Africa. Aldo's mother sent the Armenian nanny, Louisa, to us with a dish full of nuts—peanuts and almonds, walnuts and sunflower seeds—also orange juice in delicate blue glasses, still sweating with cold.

When we had demolished the peanuts and walnuts and begun on the sunflower seeds, the conversation turned to bicycles in general and my bicycle in particular. If Aldo were secretly to own a bicycle of his own, it should be possible, we decided, to keep it hidden from all suspicious eyes, at the back of the disused shed. And then, early on Saturday mornings, while his parents were still safely fast asleep, he would be able to creep out; there would be nothing to stop him riding right to the end of the world.

I pronounced expert opinions on a thousand and one relevant items, approving or disapproving of them accordingly. On spokes and valves and safety valves; on batteries as compared to dynamos; on handbrakes (which, applied at speed, would send you flying immediately) as against back pedal brakes (let them go on a downhill slope and you might as well start saying your prayers); on ordinary carriers as compared to spring carriers; on lamps and reflectors, and so on and so forth. Afterwards, we returned to the sub-

ject of the Zulu and the Bushmen and the Hottentot, what
each tribe had in common and in which way each one was
unique, and which of them was the most dangerous. I
spoke, eagerly, about the terrible Mahdi of Khartoum in
the capital city of Sudan, about the real, original Tarzan
from the forests of Tanganyika, through which I would
have to pass on my journey to the source of the River Zambezi in the land of Obangi-Shari. But Aldo was not listening any more. He was miles away, deep in his own thoughts
and seemed to grow more nervous every minute. Suddenly
he cut me short, and, in a voice high and trembling with
excitement, burst out:

"Come on! Come to my room: I'll show you something
better than you've dreamed in all your life!"

"O.K. But quick," I begged. "I've got to get started on
my journey today."

Yet, even so I followed him out of the library. To reach
Aldo's room meant traversing almost the entire length of
the Castelnuovos' house. It was very large, all its carpets
and curtains spotlessly clean, yet contriving at one and the
same time to be both faintly gloomy and a touch exotic. In
the sitting room, for instance, there was a brown grandfather clock with golden hands and square Hebrew letters
instead of numbers. There were low cupboards along the
walls and on top of them rows and rows of small antiques
made of wood or solid silver. There was even a silver crocodile, but its tail was no ordinary tail—it acted as a lever also.
If you pulled it and then pressed very lightly the crocodile
would crack nuts between its jaws for the benefit of the

Castelnuovos' guests. Moreover, the door of the passage-
way between the drawing room and the oblong dining
room was guarded balefully night and day by Caesario, a
large woolen dog, stuffed with seaweed and glowering at
you with black buttons in place of eyes.

In the dining room itself stood an enormous table made
of mahogany, wearing what looked like felt stockings on
each of its thick legs. And on the wall of the dining room
in letters of gold, this inscription appeared: *Who shall as-
cend unto the hill of the Lord? Who shall stand in His holy
place?* The answer to that question, *He who has clean hands
and a pure heart*—which happened also to be the
Castelnuovo family motto—was to be found on the opposite wall encircling the family crest; a single blue gazelle,
each of its horns a Star of David.

From the dining room, a glass door led to a little cubby-
hole called "The Smoking Room." An enormous painting
hid one wall entirely. It showed a woman in a delicate muslin dress, a silk scarf concealing all her face except for her
two black eyes, while, with one white hand, she held out to
a beggar a golden coin so bright and shining it sprayed
small sparks in all directions, like sparks from a fire. But
the beggar himself continued to sit there peacefully. He
wore a clean white cloak, his beard too was white, his eyes
closed, his face radiant with happiness. Beneath the picture
on a small copper plaque was engraved the single word,
CHARITY.

I marveled so often in this house. At Louisa, for instance, the Armenian nanny who looked after Aldo; a dark

and very polite girl of sixteen or seventeen whom I never saw without a clean white apron on top of her blue dress, both dress and apron looking newly ironed. She could talk Italian with Aldo, yet obeyed his order without question. She was also exceedingly courteous to me, calling me "the young gentleman," in a strange, almost dreamlike, Hebrew until sometimes, even to myself, I began to seem like a real young gentleman. Could she be the daughter of the woman in that great picture in the smoking room; and if not, why the likeness between them? And then, was *CHARITY* the name of the picture? Or the name of the woman in the picture? Or even the name of the painter who had painted it? Our teacher in Class Two had been called Margolit Charity. It was she who had given Aldo the Hebrew name "Alded." But who could give a name like Alded to a boy in whose house there was a room just for smoking?

(My parents' flat, with its two rooms and kitchen, separated by a short corridor, had only plain wooden tables and rush-seated chairs. Anemones or sprays of almond blossom flowered there in yogurt jars in spring, while in summer and autumn the same jars sprouted branches of myrtle. The picture on the wall of the larger of our rooms showed a pioneer carrying a hoe and looking, for no obvious reason, towards a row of cypresses.)

At the far end of the smoking room was a strange low door. We went through it and down five steps to the wing of the house which contained Aldo's room. His window looked out on the crowded red roofs of the Mea Shearim quarter, and beyond them, eastwards, onto church towers and mountains.

"Now," said Aldo, as if about to perform some kind of magic, "now, just take a look at this."

And at that, he bent down and pulled from a large and brightly patterned box, section after section of dismantled railway track, several small stations and a railway official made of tin. There followed the most marvelous blue engine, with a quantity of red carriages. Then we laid ourselves down on the floor and began to put it all together, the track layout, the signaling system, even the scenery. (It too was made of brightly painted tin; hills and bridges, lakes and tunnels; tiny cows had even been painted on the hillsides, grazing peacefully alongside the steep track.)

And when at last all was ready, Aldo connected the electric plug and the whole enchanted world sprang instantly to life. Engines whistled, coach wheels clicked busily along the tracks, barriers went up and came down again, signal lights flashed intermittently at crossings and interchanges; goods trains and passenger trains exchanging hoots of greeting, passed or overtook each other on parallel rails— magic upon magic, enchantment on enchantment.

"This," said Aldo with a slight disdain, "this I got as a present from my godfather, Maestro Enrico. He's Viceroy of Venezuela now." I was silent with awe.

But in my heart I was thinking:

Lord God Almighty. King of the Universe.

"As far as I am concerned," added Aldo with indifference, "the whole thing's pretty boring. Not to say a waste of time. Myself, I'd rather play my violin than play with toys these days. So you might as well have it. If you still play with toys, that is."

"Hallelujah, Hallelujah," my soul sang within my breast. But I still said nothing.

"Of course—," Aldo grew more precise, "—of course, I don't mean as a present. As a swap. In exchange for your bicycle. Do you agree?"

Wow, I thought to myself. Wow. And how. But out loud, I said, "O.K. Done. Why not?"

"And of course," went on Aldo immediately, "of course I don't mean the whole thing. Just one section of it in exchange for your bike; one engine, that is, five carriages and three meters of circular track. After all, your bike doesn't have a crossbar. What I'm going to do now is fetch a blank contract from Father's drawer, and if you haven't had second thoughts and changed your mind—which you still have a perfect right to do—we can sign it there and then and shake hands on it. In the meantime, you may start choosing the amount of track and the number of carriages that we agreed, plus your one engine—one of the small ones of course, not the large. I'll be back in a minute. *Ciao.*"

But I was not listening any more. I couldn't hear anything except my own heart galloping away inside my breast and bellowing out: "Shoe—shoe—shoe—shoe—shoey-shoe" (which was a nonsense song absolutely everyone was singing in those days).

In a minute the contract had been signed and I had left

the Castelnuovos' house, bursting out into Zephania Street like a train out of a tunnel, carrying carefully in front of me a shoebox gift-wrapped and tied up with blue ribbon. To judge by the light and the coolness of the air, it was half an hour or so till dusk and suppertime. I would set out the railway, I thought, in the wild and untamed landscape of our garden. I would dig a winding river, I thought, and fill it with water and make the railway cross it on a bridge. I'd raise hills and scoop out valleys, run a tunnel beneath the hanging roots of the fig tree and from there my new railway would erupt into the wilderness itself, into the barren Sahara and beyond, up to the source of the River Zambezi in the land of Obangi-Shari, through deserts and impenetrable forests where no white man had ever set foot.

4

Your Money or Your Life

In which we confront an old enemy, a bitter and cunning foe, who will stop at nothing. To avoid unnecessary bloodshed, we are obliged to fight our way through a thicket of intrigue and even to tame a young wild beast.

To judge from the fading light and cooler air, night and suppertime were approaching fast. At the corner of Jonah Street I stopped for a moment to read a new inscription on *the wall. Two mornings ago it had been empty, but here now in black paint was a fierce slogan against the British and David Ben-Gurion.** It was such a silly, irritating slogan in fact, even the spelling mistake seemed shocking.

British go hom
Get out Ben Gurion

I identified its author immediately. Goel. For this was no slogan from the Underground. This had to be the work of Goel Germanski himself. Having determined which, I took out a notebook and pencil and started to copy the inscription down. I need to make a note of everything like that, since I am going to be a poet when I grow up.

I was still standing there, writing, when Goel himself appeared. Large and silent, he crept up behind me, moving as precisely as a wolf in a forest. He grabbed my shoulders in his two strong hands and did not let me go. I did not struggle. For one thing, I don't, on principle, pick fights with boys stronger than myself. For another, I had not forgotten that I was clutching my railway, my dearest possession, in a box beneath my arm. Consequently, I needed to take particular care.

Goel Germanski was our class hoodlum, our neighbor-

---

* *David Ben-Gurion,* a leader of the Palestinian Jews opposed to British occupation, became prime minister of Israel in 1949. Goel Germanski is confused, as his "silly, irritating slogan" demands the departure of *both* Britain and Ben-Gurion.

hood hoodlum, you could say. He was very tough and muscular, the son of the deputy headmaster of our school. His mother, it was rumored, "worked in Haifa for the French." Since our heavy defeat at Purim at the hands of the Bokarim Quarter, we had been enemies, Goel and I. These days we did talk to each other, even went so far as to discuss our defeat, but always using the third person. And if I saw on Goel a certain ominous smile, I would do my best to be found on the opposite side of the street. For Goel's smile said this, approximately:

"Everyone except you knows that something very nasty is about to get you; any time now you'll know it too; all the rest of us will be laughing, only you will be laughing on the other side of your face."

Meanwhile, Goel had gripped my shoulders and asked, smiling, "So what's his little game then?"

"Please let me go," I begged politely. "It's late and I'm already supposed to be back home."

"Is that so then?" inquired Goel, letting go my shoulder. But he did not stop staring at me suspiciously, as if I had said something amazingly cunning; yet, if I had hoped thereby to fool Goel Germanski himself, then I had another think coming. That was how Goel looked at me.

Then he added very quietly:

"So he wants to go home, huh."

It was no question the way he said it. It was more as if he was pointing at some nasty aspect of my character which he was only just discovering, much to his sorrow and disappointment.

"I'm late already," I explained gently.

"Just get an earful of this," cried Goel to some invisible audience. "So he's late, huh? So all at once he wants to go home, huh? He's nothing but a dirty British spy, that's all he is. But as from right now we've got him fixed, him and his informing. As from right now we've fixed him for good."

"To start with," I corrected him cautiously, my heart pounding under my T-shirt, "to start with, I'm not a spy."

"So he isn't, is he?" winked Goel, simultaneously friendly and malevolent. "So how come he's copying that stuff from the wall, how come?"

"So what?" I inquired. And then, with a burst of courage, added: "The street doesn't belong to him. The street's public property."

"That's what he thinks," explained Goel, with a schoolmasterly patience, "that's what he thinks. Because right now he's going to start opening up that parcel of his and letting us take a good look inside."

"No I'm not."

"Open up."

"No."

"For the third and last time. He'll open up. If he knows what's good for him. That Soumchi. That scab. That dirty British spy. He'll open up, and fast, else I'll give him a hand right now."

So I untied the blue ribbon, removed the fine wrappings, revealed to Goel Germanski my railway, in all its glory.

After a brief, awed silence, Goel said, "And is he going

to tell me he got all that from Sergeant Dunlop? Just for informing and nothing else?"

"I'm not an informer. I teach Sergeant Dunlop Hebrew
sometimes and he teaches me English. That's all. I'm not
an informer."

"Then how come the railway? How come the engine?
Unless, maybe, this well-known benefactor suddenly
started handing out goodies to the poor?"

"It's none of his business," I said in the ensuing silence,
heroically.

In return, Goel Germanski grabbed hold of my T-shirt
and shook me against the fence, two or three times. He did
not shake me savagely but delicately rather—I might have
been a winter coat from which he was trying to remove dust
and the smell of mothballs.

And when he had quite finished, he inquired anxiously,
as though concerned for my welfare, "Maybe he's ready to
do some talking now?"

"O.K.," I said. "O.K. O.K. If he'll let go of me. I swapped
it. If he must know."

"He wouldn't be lying by any chance?" Goel sounded
suspicious suddenly, wore on his face an expression of the
deepest moral concern.

"Cross my heart. It's the absolute truth," I swore. "I
swapped it with Aldo. There's even a contract in my pocket
to prove it. Then he can see for himself. I swapped it for the
bike I got from my uncle."

"Uncle Wetmark," Goel pointed out.

"Uncle Zemach," I corrected him.

"A girl's bike," said Goel.

"With a lamp and a dynamo," I insisted.

"Aldo Castelnuovo?" said Goel.

"As a swap," I said. "Here's the contract."

"Right," said Goel. And thereafter looked thoughtful. We were silent for a little while. In the sky, and outside, in the courtyard, it was still daylight. But I could smell the evening approaching now. Goel broke the silence at last.

"Right," he said. "He's made one swap. Now here's another for him, if he wants. Psssst. Keeper. Here: down, sit! Sit! Right, like that. Good dog. Yes, you are. This is Keeper; he'd better take a good look at him before he makes up his mind. There's no dog like him today. Not even for fifty pounds apiece. They don't sell dogs with such pedigrees any more. His father belongs to King Farouk of Egypt; his mother to Esther Williams, in the pictures."

At Goel's shrill whistle and the sound of the name Keeper, a very young and enthusiastic Alsatian had sprung from the nearest courtyard and begun prancing all around us, panting and yelping and leaping and quivering, dancing with happiness, exploding with excitement, still so nearly a puppy he waggled his whole hindquarters, instead of just his tail. He fawned and fawned on Goel: he pressed himself against him, as if attempting to implant himself; begged his attention, to stay with him forever; flattered and beseeched him; clambered over him, his paws trembling with joy, his eyes firing sparks of wolfish love at him. In the end he was standing on his hind legs, scrabbling with all his might at Goel's stomach, until Goel checked him suddenly, with a masterful, "That's enough! Sit!"

In an instant, Keeper's lovemaking had come to an abrupt halt. His manner changed completely. He sat himself down, folding his tail neatly about him, expression thoughtful, even smug. He held his back, his head, his muzzle, as tense and still as if he were balancing a shilling on the end of his black nose. His furry ears were pricked. He was wrapped in such total gravity and humility; he looked so like a newly-arrived immigrant boy, a particularly clean and tidy boy, trying his hardest to please, it was almost impossible not to burst out laughing.

"Die," roared Goel, huskily.

Instantly Keeper prostrated himself at his feet and threw his head on his paws in eternal submission. His grief was as delicate as a poet's. His tail lay motionless, his ears were limp and totally despairing, he appeared to have ceased to breathe. Still, when Goel broke a small branch from a mulberry tree behind the fence, Keeper did not move; did not even blink an eye. And only the faintest of tremblings flowed along his back and made his grey-brown fur quiver.

But when, suddenly, Goel threw the stick into the distance and yelled, "Fetch!" in a stern voice, the dog sprang, instantly—no, did not spring, erupted—like a shower of sparks out of a bonfire, parting the air, describing four or five wide arcs on it—he might in his fury have sprouted invisible wings. His wolf's jaw opened—I caught one brief glimpse of a red-black gullet, of white teeth sharpened for the kill—the next minute Keeper was back from his errand and laying the stick at his master's feet. Then he too laid himself down in mute, even slavish submission, as if confessing that he was fit for nothing so demanded nothing, except to fulfil his obligations, naturally, for what's one caress between you and me in the end?

"Well, that's it," said Goel.

While the dog lifted his head and looked up at him with eyes full of longing and barely-concealed love, that asked:

"Am I a good dog then?"

"Yes," said Goel. "Yes, a very good dog. But you're going to change masters now. And if he doesn't treat Keeper well—," though Goel was addressing me now he still did not look at me, "—If he doesn't treat Keeper well, I'll kill him on the spot, I'll kill him; get that, Soumchi?"

He spoke these last words in a menacing whisper, his face thrust close up to mine.

"Me?" I asked, hardly daring to believe my ears.

"Yes, him," said Goel. "He's getting Keeper, as from now. And then I'll know for sure he's not an informer."

The dog was still only a puppy, though no longer helpless and no longer little. He'll obey my voice, I thought. And how. And I'll turn him back into a proper wolf, a real fierce proper wolf.

"Has he ever read *The Hound of the Baskervilles?*" asked Goel.

"Of course I have," I said. "At least twice, if not three times."

"Good. Then he'd better know this dog's been trained to tear throats out too. British cops' and spies' throats. At a word of command. And that word's the name of the King of England—I won't say it now or he'll start attacking someone here."

"Of course," I said.

"And on top of that, he'll take messages anywhere he's sent. And track down a suspect just from sniffing at one of his socks," added Goel. And after a short silence, as if he was having to take a difficult and painful decision, muttered: "Right. O.K. He gets Keeper. In exchange, that is. As a swap. Not for free. For the railway."

"But . . ."

"And if he won't, I'll show the whole class the love poem he wrote Esthie Inbar in the black notebook Aldo stole from the pocket of his windcheater in the Tel Arza wood."

"Bastards," I hissed, between gritted teeth. "Contemptible bastards." (Contemptible was a word I'd learned from Uncle Zemach.)

Goel found it expedient to ignore these epithets and preserve his good humour. "If he'll let me finish; before he starts swearing at me. Whatever that was all about. If he'll just let someone else say something. If he'll just keep his cool. He'll not only get Keeper in exchange, he'll get back his black notebook, and as well as that, he can join the Avengers, and as well as that I'll make peace with him. He only has to think a bit and he'll know what's good for him."

At that very moment a delicious haze spread through my body. Excitement gently stroked my back; there was a melting in my throat and my knees were trembling with delight.

"Hang on," I protested, at the sight of Goel beginning to untie the blue ribbons from the railway box and improvise a lead for Keeper. "Hang on, hang on a minute."

"There you are, Soumchi." Goel actually addressed me

in the second person as if we were friends again, as if nothing had happened at Purim in the battle with the Bokarim Quarter, as if suddenly I was just like anybody else.

"There you are. Grab him. Only you've got to be firm with him. He might try and escape at first, until he gets used to you. Until he does, don't let him off the lead. In a few days he'll do just what you tell him. Just do me a personal favor, though, treat him properly. And tomorrow, at three o'clock, come to the secret place on Tarzan Bamberger's roof. On the stairs you'll have to tell Bar-Kochba the password, 'Lily of the Valley,' and wait for him to answer 'Rose of Sharon,' then you'll say 'Rivers of Egypt' and he'll let you past. Because those are the Avengers' passwords. And then you'll be sworn in and then you'll get your notebook back with those poems I was talking about; I forget what they were about. Right. That's the lot. Just come tomorrow at three o'clock, or else. Go on, Keeper. Go with Soumchi. Go on, pull him, Soumchi. Pull him hard, like that. So long."

"So long, Goel," I answered, as if I really was just like anybody else, though actually, inside my head, my soul went on singing over and over like some demented songbird, "I've got a wolf, I've got a wolf, I've got a young wolf to tear out throats." But it took all my strength to drag my reluctant wolf cub after me. He dug his paws into the cracks in the pavement, protesting his wretchedness meanwhile with pathetic little whines that were beneath him altogether. So I ignored them. I just kept pulling him along. I pulled and walked and walked and pulled, while my spirit was borne far, far away, to the tangled forests and impenetrable jungles, where, surrounded, I made a brave and hopeless stand against a mob of shrieking cannibals, covered in war paint and brandishing javelins and spears. Alone and weaponless, I struck out on all sides, but for every one of them I felled with my bare hands, a host of others swarmed yelling from their lair to take his place. Already my strength was beginning to fail. But then, as my enemies closed in on me with cries of joy, their white teeth gleaming, I gave one short, shrill whistle. From out of the thicket leaped my own private wolf, menacing, merciless, rending their throats with his cruel fangs until my enemies had scattered in all directions, bellowing with fear. Then he flung himself down at my feet and lay there panting, fawning on me and looking up at me with hidden love and longing, as if to say:

"Am I a good dog?"

"Yes, a very good dog," I said. But deep in my heart I thought: This is happiness; and that's life. Here is love and here am I.

And, afterwards, darkness fell and we continued on our way through the gloom of the jungle to the source of the River Zambezi in the land of Obangi-Shari, where no white man had ever set foot, and to which my heart goes out.

5

To Hell with Everything

In which King Saul loves his father's asses and then finds a kingdom; and in which we too lose and find: and in which evening descends on Jerusalem and a fateful decision is reached.

The street was already darkening and it was growing late. Somehow I managed to drag the young wolf I got from Goel Germanski in exchange for an electric railway as far as the junction of Zephania and Malachi Streets. But there, just by the postbox, set into the concrete wall, painted bright red, with a crown raised on it and underneath the initials, in English, of King George,* the dog decided he had had enough. He pulled so hard, perhaps at the sound of some whistle I could not hear, he tore off the lead that Goel Germanski had made him out of the blue gift ribbon, so freeing himself. Then he crossed the road at a crouching run, his tail between his legs and his muzzle close to the ground, very furtive-looking, almost reptilian. Thereafter, he crept along, keeping his distance from me, as if admitting that such behavior was disgraceful. Yet, claiming too, in his own defense:

"That's how it is, mate. That's life, I'm afraid."

And then he was gone from my sight altogether, vanished into the darkness of one of the courtyards.

---

*King George. George VI was the British monarch from 1936 to 1952.

Night fell.

And so that bad dog had returned quite certainly to his real master. And what was I left with? Just one small length of the blue ribbon that Aldo Castelnuovo had tied round the box that held the railway that Goel Germanski had converted into a lead for his dog. Otherwise, I was empty-handed, and also quite alone. But that was life.

By now, I had reached the courtyard of the Faithful Remnant Synagogue (which happened to be my shortcut home, via the Bambergers' butcher's shop). I did not hurry. I had no reason to hurry any more. On the contrary. I sat down on a box and listened to the sounds about me and began to set myself to thinking. Around and around flowed the warmth and peace of early evening. I heard the sound of radios from open windows, the sound of voices, laughing or scolding. Since it no longer mattered to anyone what would happen to me—not now or all the rest of my life—it did not matter much to me what would happen to anybody else. Yet, in spite of that, I felt sorry, at that moment, because everything in the world kept changing and nothing ever stayed the same, and sorry even that this evening would never come again, though I had no reason to love this evening. On the contrary, in fact. Yet I still felt sorry for what was and would not be a second time. And I wondered if there was some faraway place somewhere in the world, in Obangi-Shari perhaps, or among the Himalayan mountains, where it might be possible to order time not to keep on passing and light not to keep on changing, just as they had been ordered by Joshua, son of Nun in the Book of Joshua. At which, someone on one of the balconies called her neighbor a crazy fool and the neighbor answered for her part, "Just look who's talking. Mrs. Rotloi. Mrs. *Rotloi*." And afterwards followed some garbled, incomprehensible sentences, in Polish maybe. And suddenly a fearful shriek rose from Zachariah Street—for a moment I hoped that Red Indians had started to attack the neighborhood already and were mercilessly scalping the inhabitants. But it was only a cat that cried and he only cried for love.

And among all the sounds of evening came the smells of evening; the smell of sauerkraut and tar and cooking oil, of souring rubbish in rubbish bins, and the smell of warm, wet washing hung out to catch the evening breeze. Because it was evening, in Jerusalem.

While I, for my part, sat on an empty box in the courtyard of the Faithful Remnant Synagogue, wondering why I should keep trying to deny it all, about Esthie.

Esthie; who is, at this moment, quite certainly sitting in her room, which I'd never seen, nor was ever likely to. And equally certainly will have drawn her two blue curtains (with which, on the other hand, I was extremely well acquainted, having looked at them from the outside a thousand times and more). And is most probably doing the homework that I have forgotten to touch, answering in her round hand the simple questions set by Mr. Shitrit, the geography teacher. Or maybe untying her plaits, or rearranging them, or maybe, very patiently, cutting out decorations for the end of term party; her skirt stretched tightly across her lap; her nails clean and rounded, not black and split like mine. She is breathing very quietly—just as in class her lips will not quite be closed and every now and then she'll be trying to reach some imaginary speck on her upper lip with the tip of her tongue. I cannot tell what she is thinking about; except that certainly she is not thinking about me. And if something does happen to remind her of me, it is most likely as "that disgusting Soumchi"; or "that crazy boy." Better, therefore, she does not think of me at all.

And, anyway, that was quite enough of that. Better for me too to stop thinking about Esthie and instead start considering, very carefully, a much more urgent question.

I began to collect up my thoughts, just as my father had taught me to do at some moment of decision. He had taught me to set down on paper all possible courses of action, together with their pros and cons, erasing one by one the least promising of them, then grading the rest according to a points' system. However, a pencil would be no use now, with daylight already gone. Instead, I listed the various alternatives in my head, as follows:

A.   I could get up and go straight home, explaining my being late and empty-handed on the grounds that my bicycle had been stolen or else confiscated by some drunken British soldier, and I had not resisted him because my mother had ordered me not to argue with the soldiers, ever.

B.   I could go back to Aldo's. Louisa, the Armenian nanny, would open the door to me and tell me to wait one moment. Then she would go by herself to announce that the young gentleman had returned and wanted a word with our young gentleman, and afterwards, very politely, she would usher me to the room where the magnificent lady in the muslin dress was presenting the beggar with a golden coin. And then I would have to confess to Aldo's mother that I had let Aldo have a bicycle, and even signed a contract for it. At which Aldo's mother would certainly punish him severely, because, under no circumstances, was he supposed to have a bicycle. And I would have behaved like a dirty low informer and not even got my bicycle back for my pains, since I no longer had the railway. Out of the question.

C. I could return to Goel Germanski. And announce in a very cold and ominous voice that he was to return the railway immediately, our contract being canceled. That he'd better give it back or I'd finish him for good. Yes, but how?

D. I could still return to Goel Germanski. But apparently friendly. "Hello, how are you, how's things?" And then ask casually if Keeper has come back to him by any chance? Yes. Of course. And tomorrow the joke will be all round the neighborhood. Total disgrace.

E. Who needs the wretched dog in any case? Who needs anything? I don't. So there. Anyway, who says Keeper fled straight back to Goel Germanski's? More likely he had run in the darkness to the Tel Arza wood and then on to the barren hills and then on to the forests of Galilee to join the rest of the pack in the wild and so to lead the life of a real free wolf at last, tearing out throats with his fangs.

Perhaps, right now, at this moment, I too could get to my feet and go to the Tel Arza wood; and from there to the hills and the caves and the winds to live as a bandit all the rest of my life and spread the fear of my name through the land forever.

Or, I could go home, tell, humbly, the whole truth, get my face slapped a few times and promise faithfully that from now on I would be a well-behaved and sensible boy instead of a crazy one. Then, straightaway, I would be dispatched with polite and apologetic notes from my father to Mrs. Castelnuovo and Mr. Germanski. I would apologize in my turn; assure everyone I hadn't really meant it; would smile a stupid smile and beg everyone's pardon; tell everyone how sorry I was for everything that had happened. Quite out of the question.

F? G? H?   Never mind. But a further possibility was simply to fall asleep among the ruins just like Huckleberry Finn in *The Adventures of Tom Sawyer*. I'd spend the night under the steps of the Inbars' house; in the very dead of night I'd climb the drainpipe to Esthie's room and we'd elope together to the land of Obangi-Shari before the crack of dawn.

But Esthie hates me. Perhaps worse than hates, she never thinks of me at all.

One last possibility. At Passover, I'd gone in Sergeant Dunlop's jeep to an Arab village and never told my parents anything. Well now, I could go to Aunt Edna's in the Yegia Capiim neighborhood, look unhappy, tell her Father and Mother had gone to Beit Hakerem this morning to visit friends and wouldn't be back till late, so they'd left me a key, and, well, I didn't quite know how to put this, only, well, I seem to have lost it, and . . . But, oh, that Aunt Edna, who wore imitation fruit in her hair and had a house full of paper flowers and ornaments and never stopped kissing me and fussing over me . . . and . . . Never mind. It would have to do. At least it solved the problem for tonight. And by to-morrow Mother and Father would be so out of their minds with worry and so thankful to see me safe and well, they would quite forget to ask what had happened to my bicycle.

Right. Let's go. I got to my feet, having made up my mind at last to beg shelter at my Aunt Edna's in the Yegia Capiim neighborhood. Only there was something glitter-ing in the dark among the pine needles. I bent to the ground, straightened up again, and there it was, a pencil sharpener.

Not a large pencil sharpener. And not exactly new. Yet made of metal, painted silver, and heavy for its size, cool-feeling and pleasant to my hand. A pencil sharpener. That I could sharpen pencils with, but also make serve as a tank in the battles that I fought out with buttons on the carpet.

And so, I tightened my fingers round my pencil sharp-ener, turned and ran straight for home, because I wasn't empty-handed any more.

Interpretive Questions

1. Why does Soumchi dream about becoming a great and noble explorer of Africa? (157, 160, 165, 175)

2. Why does Soumchi eagerly trade the bicycle that had driven him "crazy with pride and joy" for a part of Aldo's toy railway? (154, 164)

3. Why does the pencil sharpener make up for Soumchi's loss of the bicycle, railway, and dog?

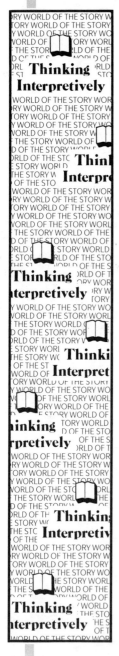

Thinking Interpretively: The World of the Story

The human conflicts and resolutions that make up the plot of a story happen in a particular world—the world that has been created by the author. In order to discover a story's full meaning, we must temporarily set aside our own opinions, histories, and values, and try to enter this world. Authors help us by providing various pieces of information, as well as vivid images that enable us to experience their worlds with all our senses. Sometimes, entering a fictional world is a matter of seeing a world very much like our own, and so we are able to experience the pleasure of recognizing a familiar setting while seeing it with new eyes. But another one of the great pleasures of fiction is being introduced to places and times different from our own. "Soumchi" is a story that combines the familiar with the not so familiar. The following questions, which we are applying to "Soumchi," can be asked of any story. As you answer these questions—giving specific, concrete answers—a clearer picture of the whole story will form in your mind.

Where does the story take place?

"Soumchi" takes place in the city of Jerusalem. More exactly, Soumchi's world consists of a neighborhood bound by specific streets, such as Zachariah, Malachi, and Zephania—names taken from the Bible. The families living in Soumchi's neighborhood are Jewish. Their names—Germanski, Castelnuovo, Weingarten—remind us that they have come there from many different countries, such as Poland, Italy, and Germany. So, although Soumchi's world is small and restricted in some ways, in other ways it is varied and unusual. And, in at least one respect, it is a troubled world, occupied by British soldiers, whom Soumchi's father calls "enemies of Israel."

When does the story take place?

The narrator, a grown-up, is writing about a time in the past, when he was "aged eleven and two months, approximately." With the help of clues in the story and a little research, we can place "Soumchi" between 1945 and 1948. Jews who had immigrated to Palestine, especially during World War II (1939-1945), wanted an independent Jewish homeland. This hope brought Jewish leaders and members of the Underground into conflict with Britain, until the state of Israel was formally declared on May 14, 1948. The action of the story falls within one day, "the day after the feast of Shavuot." This holiday occurs in mid-May and commemorates the giving of the Ten Commandments to Moses as the Israelites fled Egypt for the Promised Land. In particular, the story focuses on Soumchi's activities during a few hours between late afternoon and midnight—the period of change between day and night. When a fairly long story describes such a short period of time, we may expect that the picture of the story's world will be a richly detailed one, and this is certainly true of "Soumchi." All of these details help us to answer our next question.

What is it like to live in this world?

Throughout the story, we are given vivid impressions of Soumchi's neighborhood. With Soumchi, we marvel at Aldo Castelnuovo's fine home with its "gloomy and enticing" atmosphere, and we learn by contrast that Soumchi himself lives in a simply-furnished flat with two rooms and a kitchen. Later, sitting with Soumchi in the courtyard of the Faithful Remnant Synagogue as evening settles on Jerusalem, we hear voices "laughing or scolding," radios, and cats, and smell "sauerkraut and tar and cooking oil, . . . souring rubbish in rubbish bins, and . . . warm, wet washing hung out to catch the evening breeze."

However, the world of a story is not simply a matter of physical sensations. It also includes the attitudes, values, traditions, and problems of its people. We see that the students in Soumchi's school in Jerusalem in the 1940s tease one another and act up in class much like students nowadays. On the other hand, their everyday lives are affected by the drama of political conflict and Old Testament history. The unpopular British troops are based just down Geula Street in the Schneller Barracks; Goel Germanski bullies Soumchi by accusing him of being an informer. When he reflects on his own experiences, Soumchi compares himself to Biblical figures like Joshua or King Saul.

Reflecting on the world of a story in this way can often help us discover key themes or issues in the inner worlds of the characters—and thus bring us closer to the story's meaning. Although Soumchi is part of a close-knit ethnic community with a shared sense of history and identity, we have seen that his world is marked by conflict, both past and present. Even the Jewish holidays, as Uncle Zemach remarks, are reminders of quarrels and griefs. Like his people, Soumchi, too, has ideals and dreams—a longing for his own "Promised Land" in the land of Obangi-Shari—that make him feel at odds with his surroundings. With his new bicycle, he invites the "envy, mockery and malice" of his classmates, and then feels "great and noble" when he realizes that it is his fault "just as much as theirs" that they hate him. Being alert to the mixture of forces affecting Soumchi's life helps us to appreciate the mixed feelings he experiences throughout the story. *Why, for example, does he show his love for Esthie by doing things that will make her dislike him? Why, as he sits empty-handed and alone amid the sounds and smells of the Jerusalem evening, does Soumchi feel sorry "that this evening would never come again," though he has "no reason to love this evening"?*

Soumchi's world is not ideal. The sensations, as well as the people, are often harsh. But it is a rich and vital world. By entering into it fully, we are in a better position to share the narrator's deepest and most complex thoughts and feelings about life, and love, and change. ▮▮

Soumchi

6

All Is Lost

"We'll never set foot . . ." In which I resolve to climb the Mountains of Moab and gaze upon the Himalayas, receive a surprising invitation (and determine not to open my hand, not as long as I shall live).

Father asked softly:

"Do you know what time it is?"

"Late," I said sadly. And gripped my pencil sharpener harder.

"The time is now seven thirty-six," Father pointed out. He stood, blocking the doorway, and nodded his head many times, as if he had reached that sad but inevitable conclusion there and then. He added: "We have already eaten."

"I'm sorry," I muttered, in a very small voice.

"We have not only eaten. We have washed up the dishes," revealed Father, quietly. There was another silence. I knew very well what was to follow. My heart beat and beat.

"And just where has his lordship been all this time? And just where is his bicycle?"

"My bicycle?" I said, dismayed. And the blood rushed from my face.

"The bicycle," repeated Father patiently, stressing each syllable precisely. "The bicycle."

"My bicycle," I muttered after him, stressing each syllable exactly as he did. "My bicycle. Yes. It's at my friend's house. I left it with one of my friends." And my lips went on whispering of their own accord, "Until tomorrow."

"Is that so?" returned Father sympathetically, as if he shared my suffering wholeheartedly and was about to offer me some plain but sound advice. "Perhaps I might be permitted to know the name and title of this honored friend?"

"That," I said, "that, I am unable to reveal."

"No?"

"No."

"Under no circumstance?"

"Under no circumstance."

It was now, I knew, he'd let fly with the first slap. I shrank right back, as if I was trying to bury my head between my shoulders, my whole body inside my shoes, shut my eyes and gripped my pencil sharpener with all my might. I took three or four breaths and waited. But no slap came. I opened my eyes and blinked. Father stood there, looking sorrowful, as if he was waiting for the performance to be over. At last he said,

"Just one more question. If his lordship will kindly permit."

"What?" my lips whispered by themselves.

"Perhaps I might be allowed to see what his excellency is concealing in his right hand?"

"Not possible," I whispered. But suddenly even the soles of my feet felt cold.

"Even this is not possible?"

"I can't, Daddy."

"His highness is showing us no favor today," Father summed up, sadly. Yet, despite everything, condescended to keep on pressing me: "For my benefit. And yours. For both our benefits."

"I can't."

"You will show me, you stupid child," roared Father. At that moment, my stomach began to hurt me dreadfully.

"I've got a tummy ache," I said.

"First you're going to show me what you've got in your hand."

"Afterwards," I begged.

"All right," said Father, in a different tone of voice. And repeated suddenly, "All right. That's enough." And moved out of the doorway. I looked up at him, hoping above hope that he was going to forgive me after all. And in that very moment came the first of the slaps.

And the second. And afterwards the third. But, by then, I'd ducked out of the way of his hand and run outside into the street, running as hard as I could, bent low from sheer fright, just like Goel's dog when he ran away from me. I was in tears almost; in the process of making the dreadful decision: that I would shake the dust of that house from my feet forever. And not just of the house; of the whole neigh-borhood, of Jerusalem. Now, at this moment, I'd set out on a journey from which I'd never return. Not forever and ever.

So my journey began; but, instead of heading directly for Africa, as I'd planned earlier, I turned east, towards Geula Street, in the direction of Mea Shearim; from there I'd cross the Kidron Valley and follow the Mount of Olives road into the Judean Desert and thence to the Jordan cross-ing and thence to the Mountains of Moab, and on and on and on.

Ever since I was in Class Three or Four, my imagination had been captured by the Himalayan Mountains, those sublime ranges at the heart of Asia. "There," I'd once read in an encyclopedia, "there, among them, rears the highest mountain in the world, its peak as yet unsullied by the foot of man." And there too, among those remote mountains, roamed that mysterious creature, the Abominable Snow-man, scouring god-forsaken ravines for his prey. The very words filled me with dread and enchantment:

ranges
    roams
        ravines
            remote
                sublime, unsullied,
                    eternal snows
                        and distant peaks.

And, above all, that marvelous word: Himalaya. On cold nights, lying beneath my warm winter blanket, I would repeat it over and over, in the deepest, most reverberant voice I could drag from the depths of my lungs, Hi—ma—la—ya.

If I could only climb to the heights of the Moab Mountains, I would look east and see far away the snow-capped peaks that were the Himalayas. And then, I would leave the land of Moab and travel south through the Arabian Desert, across the Gate of Tears to the coast of the Horn of Africa. And I would penetrate the heart of the jungle to the source of the River Zambezi, in the land of Obangi-Shari. And there, all alone, I'd live a life that was wild and free.

So, desperate, and burning with eagerness, I made my way east up Geula Street to the corner of Chancellor Street. But, when I reached Mr. Bialig's grocery, one thought overcame the rest; persistent, merciless, it repeated over and over. Crazy boy, crazy boy, crazy boy. Really you are crazy, stark raving mad, bad as Uncle Wetmark, maybe even worse; for all you know you'll grow up a *spekulant,* just like him. And what exactly did the word *spekulant* mean? I still did not know.

And suddenly all the pain and humiliation seemed to well up inside me, until I could scarcely bear it. The darkness was complete now in Geula Street. Not the darkness of early evening, full of children's cries and mothers' scoldings; this was the chill and silent darkness of the night, better seen from indoors, from your bed, through a crack in the shutters. You did not want to be caught out in it alone. Very occasionally someone else came hurrying by. Mrs.

Soskin recognized me and asked what was the matter. But I did not answer her a word. From time to time a British armored car from the Schneller Barracks charged past at a mad gallop. I would seek out Sergeant Dunlop, walking his poodle in Haturim Street or Tahkemoni Street, I thought, and this time I would give him information after all; I'd tell him it was Goel Germanski who painted that slogan against the High Commissioner. And then I would go to London and turn double agent. I'd kidnap the King of England and say to the English Government straight out: "Give us back the land of Israel and I'll give you back your King. Don't give, don't get." (And even this idea came from my Uncle Zemach.) There, sitting on the steps of Mr. Bialig's grocery, I rehearsed all the details of my plan. It was late now; the hour the heroes of the Underground emerged from the hiding places, while around them, detectives and informers and tracker dogs lay in wait.

I was on my own. Aldo had taken my bicycle away and made me sign a contract to say so. Goel had expropriated my marvelous railway and the tame wolf roamed the woods and forests without me. And I was never to set foot in my parents' house again, not forever and forever. Esthie hated me. The despicable Aldo had stolen my notebook full of poems and sold it to that hoodlum Goel.

Then what was left? Just the pencil sharpener, nothing else. And what could I get from a pencil sharpener; what good could it do me? None. All the same, I'd keep it forever and ever. I swore an oath that I would keep it, that no power on earth would take it from my hand.

So I sat at nine o'clock at night—or even at a quarter past

nine—on the steps of Mr. Bialig's shuttered grocery shop and wept, almost. And so too I was found by a tall and taciturn man who came walking along the deserted street, smoking, peacefully, a pipe with a silver lid; Esthie's father, Mr. Engineer Inbar.

"Oh," he said, after he had leaned down and seen me. "Oh. It is you. Well, well. Is there anything I can do to help?"

It seemed beautiful to me, miraculous even, that Engineer Inbar should speak to me like that, as one adult to another, without a trace of that special kind of language and tone of voice that people use to children.

"Can I help you in any way?" I might have been a driver whose car had broken down, struggling to change a tire in the dark.

"Thanks," I said.

"What's the problem?" asked Engineer Inbar.

"Nothing," I said. "Everything's fine."

"But you're crying. Almost."

"No. No, not at all. I'm not crying. Almost. I'm just a bit cold. Honestly."

"All right. We're not going the same way by any chance? Are you on your way home too?"

"Well . . . I haven't got a home."

"How do you mean?"

"I mean . . . my parents are away in Tel Aviv. They're coming back tomorrow. They left me some food in the icebox. I mean . . . I had a key on a piece of white string."

"Well, well. I see. You've lost your key. And you've got

nowhere to go. That's it in a nutshell. Exactly the same thing happened to me when I was still a student in Berlin. Come on then. Let's go. There's no point in sitting here all night, weeping. Almost."

"But . . . where are we going?"

"Home. Of course. To our place. You can stay the night with us. There's a sofa in the living room, also a camp bed somewhere. And I'm sure Esthie will be glad. Come on. Let's go."

And how my foolish heart ran wild; it beat inside my T-shirt, inside my vest, inside my skin and bone. Esthie will be glad—oh, Esthie will be glad.

> *Pomegranate scents waft to and fro*
> *From the Dead Sea to Jericho.*

Esthie will be glad.

I must never lose it; my pencil sharpener, my perfect, lucky pencil sharpener that I held in my hand that I held inside my pocket.

7

One Night of Love

How only he who has lost everything may sue for hap-
piness. "If a man offered for love all the wealth of his
house . . ." And how we were not ashamed.

So there we sat at supper together, the Engineer Inbar and
I, discussing the state of the country. Esthie's elder brother
was away building a new kibbutz at Biet She'an, while her
mother must have eaten before we came. Now she set before us on a wooden dish slices of some peculiar bread, very
black and strong-tasting, together with Arab cheese, very
salty, and scattered with little cubes of garlic. I was hungry.
Afterwards we ate whole radishes, red outside, white and
juicy inside. We chewed big lettuce leaves. We drank warm
goat's milk. (At our house, that is to say the house that used
to be mine, I'd get a poached egg in the evening, with to-
mato and cucumber, or else boiled fish, and afterwards yogurt and cocoa. My father and mother ate the same, except
they finished up with tea instead of cocoa.)

Mrs. Inbar gathered up the plates and cups and went
back to the kitchen to prepare lunch for the next day.
"Now we'll leave the men to talk men's talk," she said. Mr.
Engineer Inbar pulled off his shoes and put his feet up on
a small stool. He lit his pipe carefully, and said, "Yes. Very
good."

And I tightened my fingers round the pencil sharpener
in my pocket and said, "Thank you very much."

And afterwards we exchanged opinions on matters of politics. Him in his armchair; me on the sofa.

The light came from a lamp the shape of a street lamp on a copper column, which stood in one corner beside the desk and between one wall covered in books and maps and another hung with pipes and mementoes. A huge globe stood in the room too, on a pedestal. At the slightest touch of a finger I thought it could be made to spin round and round. I could hardly take my eyes off it.

All this time Esthie remained in the bathroom. She did not come out. There was only the sound of running water sometimes from behind the locked door at the end of the corridor, and sometimes, also, Esthie's voice singing one of the popular songs of Shoshana Damari.

"The Bible," said Engineer Inbar amid his cloud of smoke, "the Bible, quite right, no doubt, of course. The Bible promises us the whole land. But the Bible was written at one period, whereas we live in quite another."

"So what?" I cried, politely furious. "It makes no difference. Perhaps the Arabs called themselves Jebusites or Canaanities in those days, and the British were called Philistines. But so what? Our enemies may keep changing their masks, but they keep persecuting us just the same. All our festivals prove it. The same enemies. The same wars. On and on, almost without a break."

Engineer Inbar was in no hurry to reply. He grasped his pipe and scratched the back of his neck with the stem. And afterwards, as if he found an answer difficult, he began gathering up from the table every stray crumb of tobacco and impounding them carefully in the ash tray. When the operation was complete, he raised his voice and called:

"Esther! Perhaps it's time you made harbor and came to see who's waiting for you here. Yes. A visitor. A surprise. No, I'm not going to tell you who it is. Come to dry land quickly and you'll see for yourself. Yes. The Arabs and British. Certainly. Canaanities and Philistines, from the day that they were born. A very intriguing idea. Only you'll have to try and persuade them to see matters in the same light. The days of the Bible, alas, are over and done with. Ours are a different matter altogether. Who on earth nowadays can turn walking sticks into crocodiles and beat rocks to make water come out? Look, I brought these sweets back last week, straight from Beirut, by train. Try one. Go on. Enjoy it. Don't be afraid. It's called *Rakhat Lokoom*.* Eat up. Isn't it sweet and tasty? And you—I assume you belong to some political party already?"

"Me? Yes," I stammered. "But not like Father . . . the opposite . . ."

"Then you support the activities of the Underground absolutely and resist any suggestion of compromise,"† stated Engineer Inbar, without a question mark. "Very good. Then we are of different minds. By the way, your school satchel with all your books and exercise books must be locked up at home in your flat. That's a pity. You'll have to

---

Rakhat Lokoom. Turkish Delight.—TRANS.

†The Zionists hoped to see all of Palestine—the Holy Land of the Bible—established as a national home for Jews. During the 1940s, they engaged in underground activities directed against British rule and the idea of compromise with the Arab population.

go to school tomorrow with Esthie, but without your satchel. Esther! Have you drowned in there? Perhaps we'd better throw you a life belt or something."

"Please could I have another piece?" I asked politely; and boldly, not waiting for a reply, pulled nearer to me the jar of *Rakhat Lokoom.* It really was delicious, even if it did come straight from the city of Beirut.

It was so good to sit here in this room, behind closed shutters, and between the walls covered in books and maps and the wall hung with pipes and mementoes, immersed in frank men's talk with Engineer Inbar. It seemed miraculous that Engineer Inbar did not snub or ridicule me, did not talk down, merely remarked, "Then we are of different minds"—how I loved that expression "We are of different minds." And I loved Esthie's father almost as much as I loved Esthie, only in a different way; perhaps I loved him more. It began to seem possible to open my heart and confess just how badly I'd lied to him; to make a clean breast of today's shame and disgrace, not even keeping from him where I was journeying to and the roads I intended to take. But, just then, at last, Esthie emerged from the bathroom. I almost regretted it—this interruption to our frank men's talk. Her hair was not in its plaits now—instead, there fell to her shoulders a newly-washed blonde mane, still warm and damp, still almost steaming. And she wore pajamas with elephants all over them, large and small ones in different colors; on her feet her mother's slippers, much too big for her. She threw a quick glance at me as she came in, then went straight over to where her father, Engineer Inbar, was sitting. I might have been yesterday's newspapers left lying on the sofa; or else I stopped there every evening on my way to the land of Obangi-Shari, there was nothing whatever in it.

"Did you go to Jericho today?" Esthie asked her father.

"I did."

"Did you buy me what I asked?"

"I didn't."

"It was too expensive?"

"That's right."

"Will you look again for me when you're in Bethlehem next?"

"Yes."

"And was it you brought him here?"

"Yes."

"What's it all about then? What's up with him?"

(I still didn't merit one word, one glance from Esthie. So I kept silent.)

"His parents are away and he lost his key. Exactly the same thing happened to me when I was a student in Berlin. We bumped into each other on Geula Street and I suggested he come to us. Mummy has already given him something to eat. He can spend the night on the sofa in the living room, or else on the camp bed, in your room. It's up to you."

Now, all at once, suddenly, Esthie turned towards me. But still without looking at me directly.

"Do you want to sleep in my room? Will you promise to tell me crazy stories before we go to sleep?"

"Don't mind," muttered my lips, quite of their own volition because I was still too stunned.

"What did he say?" Esthie asked her father a little anxiously. "Perhaps you heard what he said?"

"It seemed to me," answered Engineer Inbar, "it seemed to me that he was still weighing up the possibilities."

"Weighing-schneighing," laughed Esthie. "O.K., that's it, let him sleep in here, in the living room and be done with it. Good night."

"But Esthie," I succeeded in saying at last, if still in a whisper only, "But Esthie . . ."

"Good night," said Esthie, and went out past me in her cotton elephant pajamas, the smell of her damp hair lingering behind her. "Good night, Daddy."

And from outside in the passage, she said, "Good. My room then. I don't mind."

Who ever, before, saw a girl's room, late, towards bedtime, when the only light burns beside her bed. Oh yes, even a girl's room has walls and windows, a floor and a ceiling, furniture and a door. That's a fact. And yet, for all that, it feels like a foreign country, utterly other and strange, its inhabitants not like us in any way. For instance: there are no cartridge cases on the windowsill, no muddy gym shoes buried under the bed. No piles of rope, metal, horseshoes, dusty books, pistol caps, padlocks and India rubber bands; no spinning tops, no strips of film. Nor are there subversive pamphlets from the Underground hidden between the cupboard and the wall and, presumably, no dirty pictures concealed among the pages of her geography book. And

there aren't, wouldn't ever be in a girl's room, any empty
beer cans, cats' skulls, screwdrivers, nails, springs and cogs
and hands from dismantled watches, penknife blades, or
drawings of blazing battleships pinned up along the wall.

On the contrary.

In Esthie's room, the light was almost a color in itself;
warm, russet-colored light, from the bedside lamp under
its red raffia lampshade. Drawn across its two windows
were the blue curtains that I'd seen a thousand times from
the other side, and never dreamed I'd see from this, all the
days of my life. On the floor was a small mat made of
plaited straw. There was a white cupboard with two brown
drawers in it, and, in the shadowy gap between wall and
cupboard, a small, very tidy desk on which I could see
Esthie's schoolbooks, pencils and paintbox. A low bed, already turned down for sleep, stood between the two windows; a folded counterpane, the color of red wine, at its
head. Another camp bed had been placed ready for me, as
close as possible to the door.

In one corner, on a stool covered with a cloth, there nes-
tled a tall jug filled with pine branches and a stork made out
of a pine cone and chips of colored wood. There were two
more chairs in the room. One of them I could scarcely take
my eyes off. But the bedside lamp bestowed its quiet light
on everything alike. Russet-colored light. You are in a
girl's room, I thought. In Esthie's room, I thought. And
you just sit and don't say anything because you are just a
great big dummy. That sums it up, Soumchi, absolutely
sums it up. Which thought is not going to help me find the

right words for starting a conversation. With much agony, I managed to squeeze out the following sentence, more or less:

"My room, at home, is quite different from this."

Esthie said, "Of course. But now you're here, not there."

"Yes," I said, because it was true.

"What do you keep staring at all the time?" asked Esthie.

"Nothing in particular," I said. "I'm just sitting here . . . just sitting. Not looking at anything in particular." That, of course, was a lie. I could scarcely take my eyes off the arms of the second chair on which she'd laid the beloved white jumper, the very same jumper that, at school, I'd stuck time and again to the seat of her chair with chewing gum. Oh, God, I thought. Oh, God, why did you make me such an idiot? Why was I ever born? At this moment it would be better not to exist. Not anywhere. Not anywhere at all, except perhaps in the Himalaya Mountains or the land of Obangi-Shari, and even there they don't need such an idiot as me.

And so it was, after scraping those few words together, I sat dumb again on the folding bed in Esthie's room, my right hand still gripped tightly round my pencil sharpener and sweating a little in my pocket.

Esthie said, "Perhaps, after all, you'd rather sleep in the living room."

"It doesn't matter," I whispered.

"What doesn't matter?"

"Nothing. Really."

"O.K. If that's what you want. I'm getting into bed now

and I'm going to turn round to the wall until you've got yourself quite settled."

But I did not think of settling myself quite. Still fully dressed in my very short gym shorts and Hasmonean T-shirt, I lay under the light blanket, taking nothing off but my gym shoes which I threw as deep as possible beneath the bed.

"That's it. All clear."

"If you want, now you can tell me about the mutiny of the great Mahdi in the Sudan, just like you did to Ra'anana and Nourit and all the rest of them the day Mr. Shitrit was ill and we had two free periods."

"But you didn't want to listen then."

"But now is not then. It's now," Esthie pointed out quite correctly.

"And if you didn't listen to the story, how do you know that it was about the rebellion of the Mahdi in the Sudan?"

"I do know. Generally I know everything."

"Everything?"

"Everything about you. Perhaps even the things you think I don't know."

"But there's one thing you don't know and I won't ever tell you," I said, very quickly, in one breath and with my face to the wall and my back to Esthie.

"I do know."

"You don't."

"Yes."

"No."

"Yes."

"Then tell me and we'll see."

"No."

"That means you're only saying you know. You don't know anything."

"I know. And how."

"Then tell me. Now. And I swear I'll tell you if you're right."

"You won't tell."

"I swear I'll tell."

"Good then. It's this. That you love some girl in our class."

"That's rubbish. Absolutely."

"And you wrote her a love poem."

"You're nuts. You're mad. Stop it!"

"In a black notebook."

I would steal a thermometer from the medicine cabinet, I decided there and then. And I would break it. And, at the ten o'clock break, I'd let the mercury run out and mix a little of it with Aldo's cocoa and a little with Goel Germanski's. So that they'd die. And also Bar-Kochba's and Elie's and Tarzan Bamberger's. So that they'll all be dead, once and for all.

Esthie repeated:

"In a little black notebook. Love poems. And also poems about how you'd run away with this girl to the Himalaya Mountains, or some place in Africa—I forget the name."

"Shut up, Esthie. Or I'll throttle you. This minute here. That's enough."

"Don't you love her anymore?"

"But it's all lies, Esthie. It's all lies invented by those bastards. I don't love any girl."

"Good," said Esthie, and all at once turned out her bedside light. "That's O.K. If that's how you want it. Now go to sleep. I don't love you either."

And afterwards, while the street light slid through the cracks in the shutters and painted the room with stripes, on the table and on the chairs, on the cupboard and on the floor, on Esthie herself in her elephant pajamas, lying at the other end of the straw mat at the foot of my bed, we talked a little more. In a whisper, I confessed almost everything. About Uncle Zemach and me; about how I was like him, a crazy boy, and for all anyone knew, a *spekulant* too in the end; about what it felt like to get up and leave everything, to go in search of the source of the River Zambezi in the land of Obangi-Shari. About how I'd left all of it, the house, the neighborhood, the city, and how, in one day, I'd managed to lose a bicycle, an electric railway, a dog and even my own home. How I'd been left without anything, except the pencil sharpener I found. Till late, very late at night, perhaps about eleven o'clock, I went on whispering to Esthie and she listened to me without a single word. But then, during the silence that fell, when I'd finished my story, she said, very suddenly:

"Good. Now give me this pencil sharpener."

"The pencil sharpener? Why give you the pencil sharpener?"

"Never mind. Give it me."

"Here you are then. Will you love me now?"

"No. And now be quiet."

"Then why are you touching my knee?"

"Will you be quiet. Why does he always have to say things and make trouble? Don't say any more."

"O.K." I said. But was forced to add, "Esthie."

Esthie said, "Enough. Don't say another word. I'm going away now to sleep on the sofa in the living room. Don't say anything. And don't say anything tomorrow either. Goodnight. And anyway, there's no such place as the land of Obangi-Shari. But it's marvelous all the same that you've invented a place for just us two alone. Goodbye, then, till tomorrow."

For six weeks Esthie and I were friends. All those days were blue and warm and the nights were blue and dark. It was full, deep summer in Jerusalem while we loved each other, Esthie and I.

To the end of the school year, our love continued, and a little after, over the summer holidays. What names our class called us, what stories they told, what a joke they found it. But all the time we loved each other, nothing could worry us. Then our friendship was over and we parted, I won't say on account of what. Haven't I already written, in the prologue, how time keeps on passing and that the whole world changes? In fact, this brings me to the end of my story. In a single sentence I can tell you all of it. How once I was given a bicycle and swapped it for a railway; got a dog instead; found a pencil sharpener in place of the dog and gave the pencil sharpener away for love. And even this is not quite the truth, because the love was there all the time, before I gave the sharpener away, before these exchangings began.

Why did love cease? That is just one question. But there are many other questions I could ask if I wanted. Why did that summer pass, and the summer after? And another summer and another and another? Why did Engineer Inbar fall ill? Why does everything change in the world? And why, since we happen to be asking questions, why, now that I'm grown up, am I still here and not among the Himalaya Mountains and not in the land of Obangi- Shari?

Well then; but there are so many questions and among them some so very hard to answer. But, as for me, I've reached the end of my story—so, if anyone else can provide us with the answers, let him rise to his feet and give them to us now.

EPILOGUE
All's Well That Ends Well

Which may be skipped altogether.
I only wrote it because it is expected.

At midnight, or perhaps just after midnight, Mother and Father arrived at the Inbar family house, looking pale and frightened. Father had been searching for me since half past nine. First he had gone to inquire for me at my Aunt Edna's in the Yegia Capiim neighborhood. Then he had returned to our own neighborhood and inquired equally vainly at Bar Kochba's and Ellie Weingarten's. At a quarter past ten he had arrived at Goel Germanski's; they had awoken Goel and interrogated him closely, Goel claiming that he knew absolutely nothing. By which Father's suspicions had been aroused; he had cross-examined Goel briefly himself, and, in the course of that, the agitated Goel swore several times that the dog did belong to him and that he even had a license from the city council to prove it. Father had dismissed him at last, saying "We are going to have another little chat some time, you and I," and continued his search through the neighborhood. But it was nearly midnight before he learned from Mrs. Soskin that I had been seen sitting on the steps of Mr. Bialig's grocery, in tears, almost, and that half an hour later, Mrs. Soskin had happened to peer through her north-facing shutter and seen me still sitting there, and then, "All of a sudden, Mr. Engineer Inbar had appeared and enticed the boy away with him, by kind words and promises."

His face very white, his voice very low and quiet, Father said:

"So, here's our jewel at last; asleep in his clothes, the crazy boy. Get up please, and kindly put on your sweater that your mother has been toting round for you all evening from house to house till twelve o'clock at night. We'll go straight home now, and leave all accounts to be settled tomorrow. Forward march!"

He made polite apologies to Engineer Inbar and his wife, thanked them and begged them in the morning to thank dear Esther also (whom, as we departed, I saw briefly a long way off through the open living room door. She was tossing from side to side in her sleep, disturbed by the voices and murmuring something, probably that it was all her fault and they should not punish me. But no one besides me heard and I did not really).

Back in my bed, at home, I lay all night awake and bright and happy until the crack of day. I did not sleep. I did not want to sleep. I saw the moon depart from my window and the first line of light start gleaming in the east. And, at last, the sun setting early sparkles on drainpipes and windowpanes, I said out loud, almost:

"Good morning, Esthie."

And indeed a new day was beginning. At breakfast, Father said to Mother, "All right. As you want. Let him grow up a Wetmark. I'll just keep my mouth shut."

Mother said, "If it's all the same to you, my brother's name is Zemach, not Wetmark."

Father said, "That's all right by me. Good. So be it."

At school, by the ten o'clock break, this had already appeared on the blackboard:

In the midnight, under the moon
Soumchi and Esthie start to spoon.

And the teacher, Mr. Shitrit, wiped it all off with a duster and calmly implored as follows:

"Not a dog shall bark. Let all flesh be silent."

On his return from work on that same day, at five o'clock, the turn of the evening, Father went alone to the

Germanskis' house. He explained; apologized; made frank and complete statement of the facts; took possession of the electric railway and turned his footsteps, steadily and without haste, to the house of the Castelnuovo family. There, Louisa, the Armenian nanny, ushered him into Professor Castelnuovo's aromatic library and Father made an impartial statement of the facts to Mrs. Castelnuovo in her turn. He apologized; received apologies; handed over the railway and took possession of the bicycle. And so, at last, everything was restored to its rightful place once more.

The bicycle itself, of course, was confiscated and locked up in the cellar for three months. But I have already written how, by the end of the summer, everything had changed; how nothing stayed the same as before. How other concerns took over. But they, perhaps, belong to some other story.

Interpretive Questions

1. Why "can't" Soumchi show his father the pencil sharpener concealed in his hand? (192)

2. Why does feeling close to Engineer Inbar enable Soumchi to confide his dreams to Esthie?

3. Why does Soumchi have to go through the series of exchanges and lose everything before he can realize that "love was there all the time"? (198, 208)

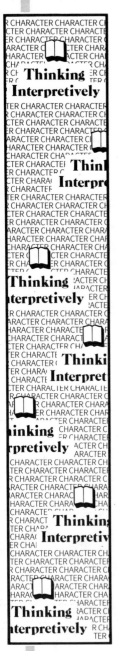

Thinking
Interpretively

Thinl
Interpr

Thinking
terpretively

Thinki
Interpret

inking
rpretively

Thinkin
Interpretiv

Thinking
terpretively

Thinking Interpretively: Character

One of the best ways we have of understanding a story's meaning is to look closely at its characters. Like people in real life, people in fiction make us want to know *why* they think, feel, and act as they do. While reading the first part of "Soumchi," for instance, we wondered why Soumchi is so eager to trade the bicycle, which at first drove him crazy with joy, for a part of Aldo's toy railway. Later, we wondered, *Why does finding a pencil sharpener make up for Soumchi's loss of the bicycle, the railway, and the dog? Why does Soumchi refuse to show the pencil sharpener to his father even though he knows he's going to be slapped?*

We are able to ask such questions because fictional characters, like real people, are

214

complex beings, with many different factors contributing to who they are and what they think and feel. Soumchi is an eleven-year-old boy experiencing his first love. He is also a Jew living in British-occupied Palestine; an only child of practical, working-class parents; and a would-be poet. Thinking about these different aspects of Soumchi helps us reach a deeper understanding of him and of the overall meaning of his story.

For instance, to begin answering the question, *Why is Soumchi obsessed with the idea of exploring Africa?* we might consider the circumstances of his family or his confused feelings about Esthie. We could also think of how the far-off land of Obangi-Shari might appeal to his poetic imagination, or how the political situation around Soumchi—of Jews longing for an independent homeland—might influence him. In this way, we begin to understand more fully Soumchi's quest to find a new and better world.

Another useful way to develop our understanding of a character is to look at that character in relation to other characters in the story. As we read "Soumchi," for instance, we found ourselves comparing him with the rest of the family and with other characters his own age, such as Aldo, Goel, and Esthie. Compared to his classmates Aldo and Goel, Soumchi seems more inexperienced, but also more sensitive, more imaginative, and certainly more likable. We aren't the only ones to make comparisons, of course. Soumchi does as well. He measures himself against his image of Esthie as near-perfect; he becomes increasingly worried that he may grow up to be just like his "crazy" Uncle Zemach. Observations like these can give us valuable insight into a character's self-image—what the character thinks about himself. With Soumchi, they help us understand why, in his moment of deepest despair—when he is running away from home after his father's beating—he hears the words "crazy boy" repeated over and over in his mind.

Besides comparing one character with others, we can also compare how the same character acts at different points in the story. At the beginning of "Soumchi," for instance, Soumchi is the class clown, the crazy boy who shows Esthie his love by tormenting her. But by the end of his day of exchanges and heartache, he opens up and confesses "almost everything" to her. Thinking about these changes in Soumchi leads us to such interpretive questions as *Why is Soumchi finally able to acknowledge his love to Esthie and to their classmates without shame? Why must Soumchi go through the series of exchanges and lose everything before he can realize that "love was there all the time"?*

Getting to know characters in fiction is much like getting to know people in real life, but with one important difference. Fictional characters are not "real"; they "live" only in the world of the story. Even though Soumchi is the narrator, he is still a creation of the author, Amos Oz. Through interpretive questions, we can ask ourselves what the author is trying to convey through his creation. We may be curious, for example, about why the two adults to whom Soumchi feels closest are so very different: the childlike "spekulant" Uncle Zemach and the dignified family man Engineer Inbar. *Why does Soumchi feel close to Uncle Zemach at the beginning of the story, but closer to Engineer Inbar at the end?* Thinking about this shift can help us gain insight not only into Soumchi's feelings, but also into what the author may be saying about growing up, searching for respect and love, and developing new ideas about what kind of people we are.

If a story is well crafted, all details about its characters are there to help tell the story and move it along to its conclusion. What is not essential is left out. We are given many details about what happened to Soumchi on one particular day and very few about what happened afterwards. But those few details are important. For instance, Soumchi tells us that his friendship with Esthie ended, but not why it did. *Why does he keep the reason to himself? Why, after pointing out that everything changes, does he let us know that he is still in Jerusalem "and not among the Himalaya Mountains and not in the land of Obangi-Shari"?*

When we ask ourselves questions such as these—when we think interpretively about character—we begin to see how the behavior and qualities of the characters point us toward the story's deeper meaning. As we read Soumchi's story, we are made to think, as he does, about the larger issue of change and the different ways we try to deal with it. ▮▮